**William Dean Howells (1837–1920).** A prolific writer of essays, fiction, nonfiction, poetry, memoirs, plays, and travel books, Howells was the gold standard of American letters from the Civil War until World War I. For many years he was the influential editor of *The Atlantic Monthly*, and from that chair befriended the likes of Mark Twain, Henry James, Bret Harte, Oliver Wendell Holmes, Ralph Waldo Emerson, and Henry Wadsworth Longfellow, all of whom, if asked, would have listed Howells as among the most influential writers of the age. He is credited with having developed a school of literature around the themes of realism. At his death he was known as the 'Lincoln of literature'. His *Italian Journeys* is also available in Tauris Parke Paperbacks.

W9-CCA-226

Matthew Stevenson is an American writer who lives in Switzerland. His *Letters of Transit: Adventures and Encounters from America to the Pacific Isles* is published by Tauris Parke Paperbacks. His most recent book is *Remembering the Twentieth Century Limited*. He is a contributing editor of *Harper's Magazine*, to which William Dean Howells contributed 335 articles between 1886 and 1920, notably for the lead column, known as the Editor's Easy Chair.

Tauris Parke Paperbacks is an imprint of I.B.Tauris. It is dedicated to publishing books in accessible paperback editions for the serious general reader within a wide range of categories, including biography, history, travel and the ancient world. The list includes select, critically acclaimed works of top quality writing by distinguished authors that continue to challenge, to inform and to inspire. These are books that possess those subtle but intrinsic elements that mark them out as something exceptional.

The Colophon of Tauris Parke Paperbacks is a representation of the ancient Egyptian ibis, sacred to the god Thoth, who was himself often depicted in the form of this most elegant of birds. Thoth was credited in antiquity as the scribe of the ancient Egyptian gods and as the inventor of writing and was associated with many aspects of wisdom and learning.

# TUSCAN CITIES

## Travels through the Heart of Old Italy

William Dean Howells

Foreword by Matthew Stevenson

TAURIS PARKE
PAPERBACKS

New paperback edition published in 2011 by Tauris Parke Paperbacks
An imprint of I.B.Tauris and Co Ltd
6 Salem Road, London W2 4BU
175 Fifth Avenue, New York NY 10010
www.ibtauris.com

Distributed in the United States and Canada Exclusively by Palgrave Macmillan
175 Fifth Avenue, New York NY 10010

Cover image: *Gateway at Siena* (oil on canvas), Dacre, Susan Isabel
(1844–1933) © Manchester Art Gallery, UK / The Bridgeman Art Library

ISBN: 978 1 84885 550 2

A full CIP record for this book is available from the British Library
A full CIP record is available from the Library of Congress

Library of Congress Catalog Card Number: available

Printed in the U.S.A.

# Contents

# *Foreword*

## *by Matthew Stevenson*[1]

For the modern traveler, the road often leads to Florence. From a cruise ship moored in Livorno, it's possible to inspect the Duomo, buy some souvenirs on the Ponte Vecchio, drink a bottle of cold water on the bus, and return to the ship in time for dinner and the floor show. Another way to see Florence is to check into one of the city's many elegant hotels, leave after breakfast with an armful of guide books, stand in long lines at the Uffizi Gallery, and finally escape to the relative calm and quiet of the Pitti Palace gardens in the late afternoon, when the setting sun, even in winter, gives Florence the light in August.

My own favorite visit to the city came after I left an overnight train at 6:30 a.m. and did all of my touring before noon, after which I ate a two-hour lunch at a local *osteria*. In the afternoon, to escape the madding crowds, I rented a bicycle and rode outside the city, in that warm Tuscan sun,

---

[1] *To my great friend,*

Peggy Brucia,

*who, beginning with my tenth grade Latin class, has taught several generations of students, and many Stevensons, to love Italy as much as she does.*

to the house where Machiavelli wrote *The Prince* and looked down on the skyline that William Dean Howells, quoting Dante, calls "the valley where never mercy is."

The key to unlocking Florence from its golden hordes is to go there with a great book, which can be read at night back in the hotel or during an afternoon rest stop in an outdoor café. Without a narrative to focus your wanderings, Florence can easily become overwhelming, a Renaissance theme park with €10 iced drinks. Few travel companions to Florence can be more engaging than William Dean Howells, an American writer of the late nineteenth and early twentieth century, who first went to Italy in 1861 as an American diplomat, stationed in Venice.

With few diplomatic chores (he had to write an annual memo on shipping traffic and entertain visiting Americans), Howells learned Italian and fell in love with the fractured country that recently had unified. His first two books were *Venetian Life* and *Italian Journeys* (available in Tauris Parke Paperbacks). In his long career he returned often to Italy, which became an emotional hometown, although one far from his roots in Ohio. He liked to say that he was "torn between two homesicknesses: the longing for America, the desire to stay in Italy."

A prolific writer of essays, fiction, nonfiction, poetry, memoirs, plays, and travel books, Howells was the gold standard of American letters from the Civil War to the First World War. For many years he was the influential editor of *The Atlantic Monthly*, and from that chair be-friended the likes of Mark Twain, Henry James, Bret Harte, Oliver Wendell Holmes, Ralph Waldo Emerson, and Henry Wadsworth Longfellow, all of whom, if asked, would have listed Howells as among the most influential writers of the age. He is credited with having developed a school of literature around the themes of realism. Writers such as F. Scott Fitzgerald, Ernest Hemingway, Theodore Dreiser, John Updike, and Edith Wharton later wrote in the style that Howells pioneered with his fiction (*The Rise of Silas Lapham*, *A Hazard of New Fortunes*, etc.) and his travel narratives, including *Tuscan Cities*. He was early in writing about business, divorce, and, on the road, in a conversational tone. He may have fallen from favor with modern readers because, with so many authors following his style – Paul Theroux and Bill Bryson are among his heirs in travel writing – his templates pale in comparison with the shinier, newer copies.

Howells came to Tuscany in 1883, to recharge his batteries after many years at the *The Atlantic Monthly* and as the high judge of American letters. He had decided to spend more time on his own fiction and essays and was drawn to the idea that a winter in Florence, Siena, and Pisa might be easier to take than those he knew so well in Boston. He also chose to return to the themes of *Venetian Life*, which is an interior view of the city seen through curious, foreign eyes.

The charm of Howells is that he is as likely to say he's bored in an art museum as he is to describe the chapel where Dante Alighieri was (unhappily) married. "To tell the truth," he confesses, "the Duomo at Florence is a temple to damp the spirit, dead or alive, by the immense impression of stony bareness, of drab vacuity, which one receives from its interior, unless it is filled with people."

What sets Howells apart from his American contemporaries – except for Mark Twain and his *Innocents Abroad* – is that he uses his travel books as rough drafts for his novels, and spends as much time examining character (as would Tolstoy, another of his favorites) as he does the cathedrals. In *Tuscan Cities*, Howells has wonderfully evocative sketches of Dante, Cosimo the Elder, Lorenzo the Magnificent, and Savonarola, who come alive on his walks across Florence, known then to only a handful of travelers. At Dante's house, struck by the village dimensions of the city, he writes: "A life of the ordinary compass witnessed so many atrocious scenes, that Dante, who peoples his Inferno with his neighbors and fellow-citizens, had but to study their manners and customs to give life to his picture."

Visiting their opulent palaces across Florence, Howells describes the vanities and brutalities of the Medici, saying of Cosimo that he is a man "capable of striking his son dead in his mother's arms," as literally happened. Moving through the family haunts, Howells writes: "From the first Medici to the last, they were nearly all hypocrites or ruffians, bigots or imbeciles; and Lorenzo, who was a scholar and a poet, and the friend of scholars and poets, had the genius and science of tyranny in supreme degree, though he wore no princely title and assumed to be only the chosen head of the commonwealth." As if in line at the Uffizi and looking down the long portico, Howells remembers the violence that has often accompanied the poetry in these houses. He reflects: "Plenty of men have been hung from its windows, plenty dashed from its turrets, slain at its base, torn in pieces, cruelly martyred before it; the wild passions of the human heart have been beaten against it like billows; it has faced every violent crime and outbreak. Yet it is sacred, and the scene is sacred. . . . "

A son of American midwestern optimism, the democratic Howells is never comfortable in the presence of old world monarchy and intrigue. The theme that elevates *Tuscan Cities* from a guide book to something more serious is the compassion that Howells shows for the death of the Florentine republic, a political experiment that he finds as uplifting as Jefferson's America. (I am sure Howells took great pleasure in his sobriquet, "the Lincoln of literature.") In his wanderings, he is quick to condemn the tyrants and eager to praise those that gave Florence the hopes of self-government. He mourns: "Yet Florence, the genius of the great democracy, never showed more glorious than in that supreme hour, just before she vanished for ever, and the Medici bastard entered the city out of which Florence had died, to be its liege lord where no master had ever been openly confessed before."

The democratic spirit leads Howells to the places in the life and death of Savonarola, the revolutionary priest who even to this day seems conjured from the fiction of Gabriel Garcia Marquez. Savonarola consigned the follies of the Medici culture to his "bonfires of the vanities." In my favorite passage, Howells describes the deathbed encounter at Villa Careggi between Savonarola and Lorenzo the Magnificent, who, negotiating until the end, tried to cajole a purgatorial pass from the austere priest, hoping that he might waive the Medici's fondness for greed and revenge. Instead Savonarola asks Lorenzo to confess the sins he has committed against Florentine democracy, which may explain why the priest himself ended up hanging in the Piazza Vecchio and was lowered onto his own conflagration. Howells's sympathies are with the doomed priest, but as an aside to the reader, he says he would rather have spent an evening with Lorenzo than with Savonarola, who might have come to dinner in his hair shirt.

Far too many people visit Florence in July, suffer in the crowds and the midday sun, and never wish to return – yet another Florentine tragedy, as beneath the overcrowded theme park, as Howells discovered, is a city as vibrant as Dante's poetry. For those heading to the city, my suggestion is to visit the Florence that interests you, but do so in a different time zone. Certainly the Italians eating dinner at 11:00 p.m. will not care. Maybe tour in the late afternoon and early evening, and then sleep until noon? Or start early, as I did, and quit before the tour buses put on their parking brakes. I would also engage Howells as your private guide. Think of each section here as an excursion and, after morning coffee, head out with him as he takes you down small alleys or into the palaces of the Medici, if not to the nearby cities of Siena or Pisa. Let his words enliven a long luncheon or share evening drinks back at the hotel. "The Florence that I saw," he concludes, "was indeed no longer the Florence of the sentimentalist's feeble desire, or the romancer's dream, but something vastly better: contemporary, real, busy in its fashion, and wholesomely and every-daily beautiful." Don't miss this chance to go abroad with a great American writer

# A Florentine Mosaic

## I.

All the way down from Turin to Bologna there was snow; not, of course, the sort of snow we had left on the other side of the Alps, or the snow we remembered in America, but a snow picturesque, spectacular, and no colder or bleaker to the eye from the car-window than the cotton-woolly counterfeit which clothes a landscape of the theatre. It covered the whole Lombard plain to the depth of several inches, and formed a very pretty decoration for the naked vines and the trees they festooned. A sky which remained thick and dun throughout the day contributed to the effect of winter, for which, indeed, the Genoese merchant in our carriage said it was now the season.

But the snow grew thinner as the train drew southward, and about Bologna the ground showed through it in patches. Then the night came on, and when we reached Florence at nine o'clock we emerged into an atmosphere which, in comparison with the severity of the transalpine air, could only be called mildly reproachful. For a few days we rejoiced in its concessive softness with some such sense of escape as must come to one who has left moral obligation behind; and then our penalty began. If we walked half a mile away from our hotel, we despaired of getting back, and commonly had ourselves brought home by one of the kindly cab-drivers who had observed our exhaustion. It came finally to our not going away from our hotel to such distances at all. We observed with a mild passivity the vigor of the other guests, who went and came from morning till night, and brought to the *table d'hôte* minds full of the spoil of their day's sight-seeing. We confessed that we had not, perhaps, been out that day, and we accounted for ourselves by saying that we had seen Florence before, a good many years ago, and that we were in no haste, for we were going to stay all winter. We tried to pass it off as well as we could, and a fortnight had gone by before we had darkened the doors of a church or a gallery.

I suppose that all this lassitude was the effect of our sudden transition from the tonic air of the Swiss mountains; and I should be surprised if our experience of the rigors of a Florentine December were not considered libellous by many whose experience was different. Nevertheless, I report it; for the reader may like to trace to it the languid lack of absolute opinion concerning Florence and her phenomena, and the total absence of final wisdom on any point, which I hope he will be able to detect throughout these pages.

## II.

It was quite three weeks before I began to keep any record of impressions, and I cannot therefore fix the date at which I pushed my search for them beyond the limits of the Piazza Santa Maria Novella, where we were lodged. It is better to

own up at once to any sin which one is likely to be found
out in, for then one gains at least the credit of candor and
courage; and I will confess here that I had come to Florence
with the intention of writing about it. But I rather wonder
now why I should have thought of writing of the whole
city, when one piazza in it was interesting enough to make
a book about. It was in itself not one of the most interesting
piazzas of Florence in the ordinary way. I do not know that
anything very historical ever happened there; but that is by
no means saying that there did not. There used, under the
early Medici and the late grand dukes, to be chariot-races
in it, the goals of which are the two obelisks by John of
Bologna, set upon the backs of the bronze turtles which the
sympathetic observer will fancy gasping under their weight
at either end of the irregular space; and its wide floor is still
unpaved, so that it is a sop of mud in rainy weather, and a
whirl of dust in dry. At the end opposite the church is the
terminus of the steam tramway running to Prato, and the
small engine that drew the trains of two or three horse-cars
linked together was perpetually fretting and snuffling about
the base of the obelisk there, as if that were a stump and
the engine were a boy's dog with intolerable conviction of
a woodchuck under it. From time to time the conductor
blew a small horn of a feeble, reedy note, like that of the
horns which children find in their stockings on Christmas
morning; and then the poor little engine hitched itself to
the train, and with an air of hopeless affliction snuffled away
toward Prato, and left the woodchuck under the obelisk
to escape. The impression of a woodchuck was confirmed
by the digging round the obelisk which a gang of workmen
kept up all winter; they laid down water-pipes, and then

dug them up again. But when the engine was gone we could give our minds to other sights in the piazza.

### III.

One of these was the passage of troops, infantry or cavalry, who were always going to or from the great railway station behind the church, and who entered it with a gay blare of bugles, extinguished midway of the square, letting the measured tramp of feet or the irregular clack of hoofs make itself heard. This was always thrilling, and we could not get enough of the brave spectacle. We rejoiced in the parade of Italian military force with even more than native ardor, for we were not taxed to pay for it, and personally the men were beautiful; not large or strong, but regular and refined of face, rank and file alike, in that democracy of good looks which one sees in no other land. They marched with a lounging, swinging step, under a heavy burden of equipment, and with the sort of quiet patience to which the whole nation has been schooled in its advance out of slavish subjection to the van of civilization.

They were not less charming when they came through off duty, the officers in their statuesque cloaks, with the gleam of their swords beneath the folds, striding across the piazza in twos or threes, the common soldiers straggling loosely over its space with the air of peasants let loose amid the wonders of a city, and smoking their long, straw-stemmed Italian cigars, with their eyes all abroad. I do not think they kept up so active a courtship with the nursemaids as the soldiers in the London squares and parks, but there was a friendliness in their relations with the population everywhere that spoke them still citizens of a common country, and not alien to its life in any way. They had leisure just before Epiphany to take a great interest in the preparations the boys were making for the celebration of that feast, with a noise of long, slender trumpets of glass; and I remember the fine behavior of a corporal in a fatigue-cap, who happened along one day when an orange-vender and a group of urchins were trying a trumpet, and extorting from it only a few stertorous crumbs of sound. The corporal put it lightly to his lips, and blew a blast upon it that almost shivered our window-panes, and then walked off with the effect of one who would escape gratitude; the boys looked after him till he was quite out of sight with mute wonder, such as pursues the doer of a noble action.

One evening an officer's funeral passed through the piazza, with a pomp of military mourning; but that was no more effective than the merely civil funeral which we once saw just at twilight. The bearers were in white cowls and robes, and one went at the head of the bier with a large cross. The others carried torches, which sometimes they inverted, swinging forward with a slow processional movement, and chanting monotonously, with the clear dark of the evening light keen and beautiful around them.

At other times we heard the jangle of a small bell, and looking out we saw a priest of Santa Maria, with the Host in his hand and his taper-bearing retinue around him, going to administer the extreme unction to some passing soul in our neighborhood. Some of the spectators uncovered, but for the most part they seemed not to notice it, and the solemnity had an effect of business which I should be at some loss to make the reader feel. But that is the effect which church

ceremonial in Italy has always had to me. I do not say that
the Italians are more indifferent to their religion than other
people, but that, having kept up its shows, always much
the same in the celebration of different faiths, — Etruscan,
Hellenic, Hebraic, — so long, they were more tired of them,
and were willing to let it transact itself without their personal
connivance when they could.


## IV.

All the life of the piazza was alike novel to the young eyes
which now saw it for the first time from our windows, and
lovely in ours, to which youth seemed to come back in
its revision. I should not know how to give a just sense of
the value of a man who used to traverse the square with a
wide wicker tray on his head, piled up with Chianti wine-
flasks that looked like a heap of great bubbles. I must trust
him to the reader's sympathy, together with the pensive
donkeys abounding there, who acquired no sort of spiritual pride from the sense of splendid array, though their
fringed and tasselled harness blazed with burnished brass.
They appeared to be stationed in our piazza while their
peasant-owners went about the city on their errands, and
it may have been in an access of homesickness too acute
for repression that, with a preliminary quivering of the tail
and final rise of that member, they lifted their woe-begone
countenances and broke into a long disconsolate bray, expressive of a despair which has not yet found its way into
poetry, and is only vaguely suggested by some music of the
minor key.

These donkeys, which usually stood under our hotel, were balanced in the picture by the line of cabs at the base of the tall buildings on the other side, whence their drivers watched our windows with hopes not unnaturally excited by our interest in them, which they might well have mistaken for a remote intention of choosing a cab. From time to time one of them left the rank, and took a turn in the square from pure effervescence of expectation, flashing his equipage upon our eyes, and snapping his whip in explosions that we heard even through the closed windows. They were of all degrees of splendor and squalor, both cabs and drivers, from the young fellow with false, floating blue eyes and fur-trimmed coat, who drove a shining cab fresh from the builder's hands, to the little man whose high hat was worn down almost to its structural pasteboard, and whose vehicle limped over the stones with querulous complaints from its rheumatic joints. When we began to drive out, we resolved to have always the worldlier turnout; but we got it only two or three times, falling finally and permanently – as no doubt we deserved, in punishment of our heartless vanity – to the wreck at the other extreme of the scale. There is no describing the zeal and vigilance by which this driver obtained and secured us to himself. For a while we practised devices for avoiding him, and did not scruple to wound his feelings; but we might as well have been kind, for it came to the same thing in the end. Once we had almost escaped. Our little man's horse had been feeding, and he had not fastened his bridle on when the *portiere* called a carriage for us. He made a snatch at his horse's bridle; it came off in his hand and hung dangling. Another driver saw the situation, and began to whip his horse across the square; our little man seized his horse by the forelock, and dragging him along at the top of his speed, arrived at the hotel door a little the first. What could we do but laugh? Everybody in the piazza applauded, and I think it must have been this fact which confirmed our subjection. After that we pretended once that our little man had cheated us; but with respectful courage he contested the fact, and convinced us that we were wrong; he restored a gold pencil which he had found in his cab; and, though he never got it, he voluntarily promised to get a new coat, to do us the more honor when he drove us out to pay visits.

## V.

He was, like all of his calling with whom we had to do in Florence, amiable and faithful, and he showed that personal interest in us from the beginning which is instant with most of them, and which found pretty expression when I was sending home a child to the hotel from a distance at nightfall. I was persistent in getting the driver's number, and he divined the cause of my anxiety.

"Oh, rest easy!" he said, leaning down toward me from his perch. "I, too, am a father!"

Possibly a Boston hackman might have gone so far as to tell me that he had young ones of his own, but he would have snubbed in reassuring me; and it is this union of grace with sympathy which, I think, forms the true expression of Italian civilization. It is not yet valued aright in the world; but the time must come when it will not be shouldered aside by physical and intellectual brutality. I hope it may come so soon that the Italians will not have learned bad manners from the rest of us. As yet, they seem uncontaminated, and the orange-vender who crushes a plump grandmother up against the wall in some narrow street is as gayly polite in his apologies, and she as graciously forgiving, as they could have been under any older régime.

But probably the Italians could not change if they would. They may fancy changes in themselves and in one another, but the barbarian who returns to them after a long absence cannot see that they are personally different, for all their political transformations. Life, which has become to us like a book which we silently peruse in the closet, or at most read aloud with a few friends, is still a drama with them, to be more or less openly played. This is what strikes you at first, and strikes you at last. It is the most recognizable thing in Italy, and I was constantly pausing in my languid strolls, confronted by some dramatic episode so bewilderingly familiar that it seemed to me I must have already attempted to write about it. One day, on the narrow sidewalk beside the escutcheoned cloister-wall of the church, two young and handsome people stopped me while they put upon that public stage the pretty melodrama of their feelings. The bare-headed girl wore a dress of the red and black plaid of the Florentine laundresses, and the young fellow standing beside her had a cloak falling from his left shoulder. She was looking down and away from him, impatiently pulling with one hand at the fingers of another, and he was vividly gesticulating, while he explained or expostulated, with his eyes not upon her, but looking straight forward; and they both stood as if, in a moment of opera, they were confronting an audience over the footlights. But they were both quite unconscious, and were merely obeying the histrionic instinct of their race. So was the school-boy in clerical robes, when, goaded by some taunt, pointless to the foreign bystander, he flung himself into an attitude of deadly scorn, and defied the tormenting *gamins;* so were the vender of chestnut-paste and his customer, as they debated over the smoking viand the exact quantity and quality which a *soldo* ought to purchase, in view of the state of the chestnut market and the price demanded elsewhere; so was the little woman who deplored, in impassioned accents, the non-arrival of the fresh radishes we liked with our coffee, when I went a little too early for them to her stall; so was the fruiterer who called me back with an effect of heroic magnanimity to give me the change I had forgotten, after beating him down from a franc to seventy centimes on a dozen of mandarin oranges. The sweetness of his air, tempering the severity of his self-righteousness in doing this, lingers with me yet, and makes me ashamed of having got the oranges at a just price. I wish he had cheated me.

We, too, can be honest if we try, but the effort seems to sour most of us. We hurl our integrity in the teeth of the person whom we deal fairly with; but when the Italian makes up his mind to be just, it is in no ungracious spirit. It was their lovely ways, far more than their monuments of history and art, that made return to the Florentines delightful. I would rather have had a perpetuity of the *cameriere's* smile when he came up with our coffee in the morning than Donatello's San Giorgio, if either were purchasable; and the face of the old chamber-maid, Maria, full of motherly affection, was better than the façade of Santa Maria Novella.

## VI.

It is true that the church bore its age somewhat better; for though Maria must have been beautiful, too, in her youth, her complexion had not that luminous flush in which three hundred years have been painting the marble front of the church. It is this light, or this color, – I hardly know which to call it, – that remains in my mind as the most characteristic quality of Santa Maria Novella; and I would like to have it go as far as possible with the reader, for I know that the edifice would not otherwise present itself in my pages, however flatteringly entreated or severely censured. I remember the bold mixture of the styles in its architecture, the lovely sculptures of its grand portals, the curious sun-dials high in its front; I remember the brand-new restoration of the screen of monuments on the right, with the arms of the noble patrons of the church carved below them, and the grass of the space enclosed showing green through the cloister-arches all winter long; I remember also the unemployed laborers crouching along its sunny base for the heat publicly dispensed in Italy on bright days – when it is not needed; and they all gave me the same pleasure, equal in degree, if not in kind. While the languor of these first days was still heavy upon me, I crept into the church for a look at the Ghirlandajo frescos behind the high altar, the Virgin of Cimabue, and the other objects which one is advised to see there, and had such modest satisfaction in them as may come to one who long ago, once for all, owned to himself that emotions to which others testified in the presence of such things were beyond him. The old masters and their humble acquaintance met shyly, after so many years; these were the only terms

on which I, at least, could preserve my self-respect; and
it was not till we had given ourselves time to overcome
our mutual diffidence that the spirit in which their work
was imagined stole into my heart and made me thoroughly
glad of it again. Perhaps the most that ever came to me
was a sense of tender reverence, of gracious quaintness in
them; but this was enough. In the mean while I did my duty
in Santa Maria Novella. I looked conscientiously at all the
pictures, in spite of a great deal of trouble I had in putting on
my glasses to read my "Walks in Florence" and taking them
off to see the paintings; and I was careful to identify the
portraits of Poliziano and the other Florentine gentlemen
and ladies in the frescos. I cannot say that I was immediately
sensible of advantage in this achievement; but I experienced
a present delight in the Spanish chapel at finding not only
Petrarch and Laura, but Boccaccio and Fiammetta, in the
groups enjoying the triumphs of the church militant. It will
always remain a confusion in our thick Northern heads, this
attribution of merit through mere belief to people whose
lives cast so little lustre on their creeds; but the confusion
is an agreeable one, and I enjoyed it as much as when it first
overcame me in Italy.

### VII.

The cicerone who helped me about these figures was a
white-robed young monk, one of twelve who are still left
at Santa Maria Novella to share the old cloisters now mainly
occupied by the pupils of a military college and a children's
school. It was noon, and the corridors and the court were
full of boys at their noisy games, on whom the young father

smiled patiently, lifting his gentle voice above their clamor to speak of the suppression of the convents. This was my first personal knowledge of the effect of that measure, and I now perceived the hardship which it must have involved, as I did not when I read of it, with my Protestant satisfaction, in the newspapers. The uncomfortable thing about any institution which has survived its usefulness is that it still embodies so much harmless life that must suffer in its destruction. The monks and nuns had been a heavy burden no doubt, for many ages, and at the best they cumbered the ground; but when it came to a question of sweeping them away, it meant sorrow and exile and dismay to thousands of gentle and blameless spirits like the brother here, who recounted one of many such histories so meekly, so unresentfully. He and his few fellows were kept there by the piety of certain faithful who, throughout Italy, still maintain a dwindling number of monks and nuns in their old cloisters wherever the convent happened to be the private property of the order. I cannot say that they thus quite console the sentimentalist who would not have the convents re-established, even while suffering a poignant regret for their suppression; but I know from myself that this sort of sentimentalist is very difficult, and perhaps he ought not to be too seriously regarded.

## VIII.

The sentimentalist is very abundant in Italy, and most commonly he is of our nice and religion, though he is rather English than American. The Englishman, so chary of his sensibilities at home, abandons himself to them abroad. At Rome he already regrets the good old days of the temporal

power, when the streets were unsafe after nightfall and un-
clean the whole twenty-four hours, and there was no new
quarter. At Venice he is bowed down under the restorations
of the Ducal Palace and the church of St. Mark; and he has
no language in which to speak of the little steamers on the
Grand Canal, which the Venetians find so convenient. In
Florence, from time to time, he has a panic prescience that
they are going to tear down the Ponte Vecchio. I do not
know how he gets this, but he has it, and all the rest of us
sentimentalists eagerly share it with him when he comes in
to the *table d'hôte* luncheon, puts his Baedeker down by his
plate, and before he has had a bite of anything calls out:
"Well, they are going to tear down the Ponte Vecchio!"

The first time that this happened in our hotel, I was still
under the influence of the climate; but I resolved to visit
the Ponte Vecchio with no more delay, lest they should
be going to tear it down that afternoon. It was not that I
cared a great deal for the bridge itself, but my accumulating
impressions of Florentine history had centred about it as the
point where that history really began to be historic. I had
formed the idea of a little dramatic opening for my sketches
there, with Buondelmonte riding in from his villa to meet his
bride, and all that spectral train of Ghibelline and Guelphic
tragedies behind them on the bridge; and it appeared to me
that this could not be managed if the bridge were going to
be torn down. I trembled for my cavalcade, ignominiously
halted on the other side of the Arno, or obliged to go round
and come in on some other bridge without regard to the
fact; and at some personal inconvenience I hurried off to
the Ponte Vecchio. I could not see that the preparations
for its destruction had begun, and I believe they are still

threatened only in the imagination of sentimental Anglo-Saxons. The omnibuses were following each other over the bridge in the peaceful succession of so many horse-cars to Cambridge, and the ugly little jewellers' booths glittered in their wonted security on either hand all the way across. The carriages, the carts, the foot-passengers were swarming up and down from the thick turmoil of Por San Maria; and the bridge did not respond with the slightest tremor to the heel clandestinely stamped upon it for a final test of its stability.

But the alarm I had suffered was no doubt useful, for it was after this that I really began to be serious with my material, as I found it everywhere in the streets and the books, and located it from one to the other. Even if one has no literary designs upon the facts, that is incomparably the best way of dealing with the past. At home, in the closet, one may read history, but one can realize it, as if it were something personally experienced, only on the spot where it was lived. This seems to me the prime use of travel; and to create the reader a partner in the enterprise and a sharer in its realization seems the sole excuse for books of travel, now when modern facilities have abolished hardship and danger and adventure, and nothing is more likely to happen to one in Florence than in Fitchburg.

In this pursuit of the past, the inquirer will often surprise himself in the possession of a genuine emotion; at moments the illustrious or pathetic figures of other days will seem to walk before him unmocked by the grotesque and bur lesquing shadows we all cast while in the flesh. I will not swear it, but it would take little to persuade me that I had vanishing glimpses of many of these figures in Florence. One of the advantages of this method is that you have your

historical personages in a sort of picturesque contemporane-
ity with one another and with yourself, and you imbue them
all with the sensibilities of our own time. Perhaps this is not
an advantage, but it shows what may be done by the imag-
inative faculty; and if we do not judge men by ourselves,
how are we to judge them at all?

## IX.

I took some pains with my Florentines, first and last, I will
confess it. I went quite back with them to the lilies that
tilted all over the plain where they founded their city in
the dawn of history, and that gave her that flowery name of
hers. I came down with them from Fiesole to the first marts
they held by the Arno for the convenience of the merchants
who did not want to climb that long hill to the Etruscan
citadel; and I built my wooden hut with the rest hard by the
Ponte Vecchio, which was an old bridge a thousand years
before Gaddi's structure. I was with them all through that
dim turmoil of wars, martyrdoms, pestilences, heroisms,
and treasons for a thousand years, feeling their increas-
ing purpose of municipal freedom and hatred of the one-
man power (*il governo d'un solo*) alike under Romans, Huns,
Longobards, Franks, and Germans, till in the eleventh century they marched up against their mother city, and destroyed Fiesole, leaving nothing standing but the fortress,
the cathedral, and the Caffè Aurora, where the visitor
lunches at this day, and has an incomparable view of Florence in the distance. When, in due time, the proud citizens
began to go out from their gates and tumble their castles
about the ears of the Germanic counts and barons in the
surrounding country, they had my sympathy almost to the

point of active co-operation; though I doubt now if we did well to let those hornets come into the town and build other nests within the walls, where they continued nearly as pestilent as ever. Still, so long as no one of them came to the top permanently, there was no danger of the one-man power we dreaded, and we could adjust our arts, our industries, our finances to the state of street warfare, even if it lasted, as at one time, for forty years. I was as much opposed as Dante himself to the extension of the national limits, though I am not sure now that our troubles came from acquiring territory three miles away, beyond the Ema, and I could not trace the bitterness of partisan feeling even to the annexation of Prato, whither it took me a whole hour to go by the steam-tram. But when the factions were divided under the names of Guelph and Ghibelline, and subdivided again into Bianchi and Neri, I was always of the Guelph and the Bianchi party, for it seemed to me that these wished the best to the commonwealth, and preserved most actively the traditional fear and hate of the one-man power. I believed heartily in the wars against Pisa and Siena, though afterward, when I visited those cities, I took their part against the Florentines, perhaps because they were finally reduced by the Medici — a family I opposed from the very first, uniting with any faction or house that contested its rise. They never deceived me when they seemed to take the popular side, nor again when they voluptuously favored the letters and arts, inviting the city full of Greeks to teach them. I mourned all through the reign of Lorenzo the Magnificent over the subjection of the people, never before brought under the one-man power, and flattered to their undoing by the splendors of the city and the state he created for him. When our dissolute youth went singing his obscene songs through the moonlit streets,

I shuddered with a good Piagnone's abhorrence; and I heard one morning with a stern and solemn joy that the great Frate had refused absolution to the dying despot who had refused freedom to Florence. Those were great days for one of my thinking, when Savonarola realized the old Florentine ideal of a free commonwealth, with the Medici banished, the Pope defied, and Christ king; days incredibly dark and terrible, when the Frate paid for his good-will to us with his life, and suffered by the Republic which he had restored. Then the famous siege came, the siege of fifteen months, when Papist and Lutheran united under one banner against us, and treason did what all the forces of the Empire had failed to effect. Yet Florence, the genius of the great democracy, never showed more glorious than in that supreme hour, just before she vanished forever, and the Medici bastard entered the city out of which Florence had died, to be its liege lord where no master had ever been openly confessed before. I could follow the Florentines intelligently through all till that; but then, what suddenly became of that burning desire of equality, that deadly jealousy of a tyrant's domination, that love of country surpassing the love of life? It is hard to reconcile ourselves to the belief that the right can be beaten, that the spirit of a generous and valiant people can be broken; but this is what seems again and again to happen in history, though never so signally, so spectacularly, as in Florence when the Medici were restored. After that there were conspiracies and attempts of individuals to throw off the yoke; but in the great people, the prostrate body of the old democracy, not a throe of revolt. Had they outlived the passion of their youth for liberty, or were they sunk in despair before the odds arrayed against them? I did not know what to do with the Florentines from this point;

they mystified me, silently suffering under the Medici for two hundred years, and then sleeping under the Lorrainese for another century, to awake in our own time the most polite, the most agreeable of the Italians perhaps, but the most languid. They say of themselves, "We lack initiative;" and the foreigner most disposed to confess his ignorance cannot help having heard it said of them by other Italians that while the Turinese, Genoese, and Milanese, and even the Venetians, excel them in industrial enterprise, they are less even than the Neapolitans in intellectual activity; and that when the capital was removed to Rome they accepted adversity almost with indifference, and resigned themselves to a second place in everything. I do not know whether this is true; there are some things against it, as that the Florentine schools are confessedly the best in Italy, and that it would be hard anywhere in that country or another to match the group of scholars and writers who form the University of Florence. These are not all Florentines, but they live in Florence, where almost any one would choose to live if he did not live in London, or Boston, or New York, or Helena, Montana T. There is no more comfortable city in the world, I fancy. But you cannot paint comfort so as to interest the reader of a book of travel. Even the lack of initiative in a people who conceal their adversity under very good clothes, and have abolished beggary, cannot be made the subject of a graphic sketch; one must go to their past for that.

## X.

Yet if the reader had time, I would like to linger a little on our way down to the Via Borgo Santi Apostoli, where it branches off into the Middle Ages out of Via Tornabuoni, not far from Vieusseux's Circulating Library. For Via Tornabuoni *is* charming, and merits to be observed for the ensemble it offers of the contemporary Florentine expression, with its alluring shops, its confectioners and cafés, its florists and milliners, its dandies and tourists, and, ruggedly massing up out of their midst, the mighty bulk of its old Strozzi Palace, mediæval, sombre, superb, tremendously impressive of the days when really a man's house was his castle. Everywhere in Florence the same sort of contrast presents itself in some degree; but nowhere quite so dramatically as here, where it seems expressly contrived for the sensation of the traveller when he arrives at the American banker's with his letter of credit the first morning, or comes to the British pharmacy for his box of quinine pills. It is eminently the street of the tourists, who are always haunting it on some errand. The best shops are here, and the most English is spoken; you hear our tongue spoken almost as commonly as Italian and much more loudly, both from the chest and through the nose, whether the one is advanced with British firmness to divide the groups of civil and military loiterers on the narrow pavement before the confectioner Giacosa's, or the other is flattened with American curiosity against the panes of the jewellers' windows. There is not here the glitter of mosaics which fatigues the eye on the Lungarno or in Via Borgognissanti, nor the white glare of new statuary – or statuettary, rather – which renders other streets impassable; but there is a sobered richness in the display, and a local character in the prices which will sober the purchaser.

Florence is not well provided with spaces for the out-door lounging which Italian leisure loves, and you must go to the Cascine for much Florentine fashion if you want it; but

something of it is always rolling down through Via
Tornabuoni in its carriage at the proper hour of the day,
and something more is always standing before Giacosa's,
English-tailored, Italian-mannered, to bow, and smile, and
comment. I was glad that the sort of swell whom I used to
love in the Piazza at Venice abounded in the narrower limits
of Via Tornabuoni. I was afraid he was dead; but he graced
the curbstone there with the same lily-like disoccupation and
the same sweetness of aspect which made the Procuratie.
Nuove like a garden. He was not without his small dog or his
cane held to his mouth; he was very, very patient and kind
with the aged crone who plays the part of Florentine flower-
girl in Via Tornabuoni, and whom I after saw aiming with
uncertain eye a *boutonnière* of violets at his coat-lapel; there
was the same sort of calm, heavy-eyed beauty looking out at
him from her ice or coffee through the vast pane of the confectioner's window, that stared sphinx-like in her mystery
from a cushioned corner of Florian's; and the officers went
by with tinkling spurs and sabres, and clicking boot-heels,
differing in nothing but their Italian uniforms and com-
plexions from the blonde Austrian military of those far-off
days. I often wondered who or what those beautiful swells
might be, and now I rather wonder that I did not ask some
one who could tell me. But perhaps it was not important;
perhaps it might even have impaired their value in the picture
of a conscientious artist who can now leave them, without
a qualm, to be imagined as rich and noble as the reader
likes. Not all the frequenters of Doney's famous café were
both, if one could trust hearsay. Besides those who could
afford to drink the first sprightly runnings of his coffee-pot,
it was said that there was a genteel class, who, for the sake

of being seen to read their newspapers there, paid for the second decantation from its grounds, which comprised what was left in the cups from the former. This might be true of a race which loves a goodly outside perhaps a little better than we do; but Doney's is not the Doney's of old days, nor its coffee so very good at first hand. Yet if that sort of self-sacrifice goes on in there, I do not object; it continues the old Latin tradition of splendor and hunger which runs through so many pleasant books, and is as good in its way as a beggar at the gate of a palace. It is a contrast; it flatters the reader who would be incapable of it; and let us have it. It is one of the many contrasts in Florence which I spoke of, and not all of which there is time to point out. But if you would have the full effect of the grimness and rudeness of the Strozzi Palace (drolly parodied, by the way, in a structure of the same street which is like a Strozzi Palace on the stage), look at that bank of flowers at one corner of its base — roses, carnations, jonquils, great Florentine anemones — laying their delicate cheeks against the savage blocks of stone, rent and burst from their quarry, and set here with their native rudeness untamed by hammer or chisel.

## XI.

The human passions were wrought almost as primitive into the civic structure of Florence, down in the thirteenth century, which you will find with me at the bottom of the Borgo Santi Apostoli, if you like to come. There and thereabouts dwelt the Buondelmonti, the Amidei, the Uberti, the Lamberti, and other noble families, in fastnesses of stone and iron as formidable as the castles from which their ancestors were dislodged when the citizens went out into the country around Florence, and destroyed their strongholds and obliged them to come into the city; and thence from their casements and towers they carried on their private wars as conveniently as ever, descending into the streets, and battling about among the peaceful industries of the vicinity for generations. It must have been inconvenient for the industries, but so far as one can understand, they suffered it just as a Kentucky community now suffers the fighting out of a family feud in its streets, and philosophically gets under shelter when the shooting begins. It does not seem to have been objected to some of these palaces that they had vaulted passageways under their first stories, provided with trap-doors to let the besieged pour hot water down on the passers below; these avenues were probably strictly private, and the citizens did not use them at times when family feeling ran high. In fact, there could have been but little coming and going about these houses for any who did not belong in them. A whole quarter, covering the space of several American city blocks, would be given up to the palaces of one family and its adherents, in a manner which one can hardly understand without seeing it. The Peruzzi, for example, enclosed a Roman amphitheatre with their palaces, which still follow in structure the circle of the ancient edifice; and the Peruzzi were rather peaceable people, with less occasion for fighting-room than many other Florentine families, — far less than the Buondelmonti, Uberti, Amidei, Lamberti, Gherardini, and others, whose domestic fortifications seem to have occupied all that region lying near the end of the Ponte Vecchio. They used to fight from their

towers on three corners of Por San Maria above the heads
of the people passing to and from the bridge, and must have
occasioned a great deal of annoyance to the tourists of that
day. Nevertheless, they seem to have dwelt in very tolerable
enmity together till one day when a Florentine gentleman
invited all the noble youth of the city to a banquet at his
villa, where, for their greater entertainment, there was a
buffoon playing his antics. This poor soul seems not to have
been a person of better taste than some other humorists,
and he thought it droll to snatch away the plate of Uberto
degl' Infangati, who had come with Buondelmonte, at which
Buondelmonte became furious, and resented the insult to
his friend, probably in terms that disabled the politeness of
those who laughed, for it is recorded that Oddo di Arrigo
dei Fifanti, "a proud and resolute man," became so incensed
as to throw a plate and its contents into Uberto's face. The
tables were overturned, and Buondelmonte stabbed Oddo
with a knife; at which point the party seems to have broken
up, and Oddo returned to Florence from Campi, where
the banquet was given, and called a family council to plot
vengeance. But a temperate spirit prevailed in this senate,
and it was decided that Buondelmonte, instead of dying,
should marry Oddo's niece, Beparata degli Amidei, differ-
ently described by history as a plain girl, and as one of the
most beautiful and accomplished damsels of the city, of a
very noble and consular family. Buondelmonte, a handsome
and gallant cavalier, but a weak will, as appears from all that
happened, agreed to this, and everything was happily arranged, till one day when he was riding by the house of
Forese Donati. Monna Gualdrada Donati was looking out
of the window, and possibly expecting the young man. She

called to him, and when he had alighted and come into the house she began to mock him.

"Cheer up, young lover! Your wedding-day is coming, and you will soon be happy with your bride."

"You know very well," said Buondelmonte, "that this marriage was a thing I could not get out of."

"Oh, indeed !" cried Monna Gualdrada. "As if you did not care for a pretty wife!" And then it was, we may suppose, that she hinted those things she is said to have insinuated against Reparata's looks and her fitness otherwise for a gentleman like Buondelmonte. "If I had known you were in such haste to marry – but God's will be done! We cannot have things as we like in this world!" And Machiavelli says that the thing Monna Gualdrada had set her heart on was Buondelmonte's marriage with her daughter, "but either through carelessness, or because she thought it would do any time, she had not mentioned it to any one." She added, probably with an affected carelessness, that the Donati were of rather better lineage than the Amidei, though she did not know whether he would have thought her Beatrice as pretty as Reparata. Then suddenly she brought him face to face with the girl, radiantly beautiful, the most beautiful in Florence. "This is the wife I was keeping for you," said Monna Gualdrada; and she must have known her ground well, for she let the poor young man understand that her daughter had long been secretly in love with him. Malespini tells us that Buondelmonte was tempted by a diabolical spirit to break faith at this sight; the devil accounted for a great many things then to which we should not now, perhaps, assign so black an origin. "And I would very willingly marry her," he faltered, "if I were not bound by that solemn promise to the Amidei;"

and Monna Gualdrada now plied the weak soul with such
arguments and reasons, in such wise as women can use them,
that he yielded, and giving his hand to Beatrice, he did not
rest till they were married. Then the Amidei, the Uberti,
the Lamberti, and the Fifanti, and others who were outraged
in their cousinship or friendship by this treachery and insult
to Reparata, assembled in the church of Santa Maria sopra
Porta to take counsel again for vengeance. Some were of
opinion that Buondelmonte should be cudgelled, and thus
publicly put to shame; others that he should be wounded
and disfigured in the face; but Mosca Lamberti rose and said:
"There is no need of all these words. If you strike him or
disfigure him, get your graves ready to hide in. *Cosa fatta
capo ha!*" With which saying he advised them to make an end
of Buondelmonte altogether. His words had the acceptance
that they would now have in a Kentucky family council, and
they agreed to kill Buondelmonte when he should come to
fetch home his bride. On Easter morning, in the year 1215,
they were waiting for him in the house of the Amidei, at the
foot of the Ponte Vecchio; and when they saw him come
riding, richly dressed in white, on a white palfrey, over the
bridge, and "fancying," says Machiavelli, "that such a wrong
as breaking an engagement could be so easily forgotten,"
they sallied out to the statue of Mars which used to be there.
As Buondelmonte reached the group, – it must have been,
for all his courage, with a face as white as his mantle, –
Schiatta degli Uberti struck him on the head with a stick,
so that he dropped stunned from his palfrey. Then Oddo di
Arrigo, whom he had stabbed, and Mosca Lamberti, who
had pronounced his sentence, and Lambertaccio Amidei,
"and one of the Gangolandi," ran and cut his throat.

There arose a terrible tumult in the city, and the girl whose fatal beauty had wrought this horror, governing herself against her woman's weakness with supernatural strength, mounted the funeral car beside her lover's body, and taking his head into her lap, with his blood soaking her bridal robes, was drawn through the city everywhere, crying for vengeance.

From that hour, they tell us, the factions that had long tormented Florence took new names, and those who had sided with the Buondelmonti and the Donati for the Pope against the Emperor became Guelphs, while the partisans of the Amidei and the Empire became Ghibellines, and began that succession of reciprocal banishments which kept a good fourth of the citizens in exile for three hundred years.

## XII.

What impresses one in this and the other old Florentine stories is the circumstantial minuteness with which they are told, and their report has an air of simple truth very different from the literary factitiousness which one is tempted to in following them. After six centuries the passions are as living, the characters as distinct, as if the thing happened yesterday. Each of the persons stands out a very man or woman, in that clear, strong light of the early day which they move through. From the first the Florentines were able to hit each other off with an accuracy which comes of the southern habit of living much together in public, and one cannot question these lineaments. Buondelmonte, Mosca Lamberti, Monna Gualdrada, and even that "one of the Gangolandi," how they possess the imagination! Their palaces still rise there in the grim, narrow streets, and seem no older in that fine Florentine air than houses of fifty years ago elsewhere. They were long since set apart, of course, to other uses. The chief palace of the Buondelmonti is occupied by an insurance company; there is a little shop for the sale of fruit and vegetables niched into the grand Gothic portal of the tower, and one is pushed in among the pears and endives by the carts which take up the whole street from wall to wall in passing. The Lamberti palace was confiscated by the Guelph party, and was long used by the Art of Silk for its guild meetings. Now it is a fire-engine house, where a polite young lieutenant left his architectural drawings to show us some frescos of Giotto lately uncovered there over an old doorway. Over a portal outside the arms of the guild were beautifully carved by Donatello, as you may still see; and in a lofty angle of the palace the exquisite loggia of the family shows its columns and balustrade against the blue sky.

I say blue sky for the sake of the color, and because that is expected of one in mentioning the Florentine sky; but, as a matter of fact, I do not believe it was blue half a dozen days during the winter of 1882–83. The prevailing weather was gray, and down in the passages about the bases of these mediæval structures the sun never struck, and the point of the mediæval nose must always have been very cold from the end of November till the beginning of April.

The tradition of an older life continues into the present everywhere; only in Italy it is a little more evident, and one realizes in the discomfort of the poor, who have succeeded to these dark and humid streets, the discomfort of the rich who once inhabited them, and whose cast-off manners have been left there. Monna Gualdrada would not now call out to Buondelmonte riding under her window, and make him come in and see her beautiful daughter; but a woman of the class which now peoples the old Donati houses might do it.

I walked through the Borgo Santi Apostoli for the last time late in March, and wandered round in the winter, still lingering in that wonderful old nest of palaces, before I came out into the cheerful bustle of Por San Maria, the street which projects the glitter of its jewellers' shops quite across the Ponte Vecchio. One of these, on the left corner, just before you reach the bridge, is said to occupy the site of the loggia of the Amidei; and if you are young and strong, you may still see them waiting there for Buondelmonte. But my eyes are not very good any more, and I saw only the amiable modern Florentine crowd, swollen by a vast number of English and American tourists, who at this season begin to come up from Rome. There are a good many antiquarian and bricabrac shops in Por San Maria; but the towers which the vanished families used to fight from have been torn down, so that there is comparatively little danger from a chance bolt there.

## XIII.

One of the furious Ghibelline houses of this quarter were the Gherardini, who are said to have become the Fitzgeralds of Ireland, whither they went in their exile, and where they enjoyed their fighting privileges long after those of their friends and acquaintances remaining in Florence had been cut off. The city annals would no doubt tell us what end the Amidei and the Lamberti made; from the Uberti came the great Farinata, who, in exile with the other Ghibellines, refused with magnificent disdain to join them in the destruction of Florence. But the history of the Buondelmonti has become part of the history of the world. One branch of the family migrated from Tuscany to Corsica, where they changed their name to Buonaparte, and from them came the great Napoleon. As to that "one of the Gangolandi," he teases me into vain conjecture, lurking in the covert of his family name, an elusive personality which I wish some poet would divine for us. The Donati afterward made a marriage which brought them into as lasting remembrance as the Buondelmonti; and one visits their palaces for the sake of Dante rather than Napoleon. They enclose, with the Alighieri house in which the poet was born, the little Piazza Donati, which you reach by going up the Corso to the Borgo degli Albizzi, and over against them on that street the house of the Portinari stood, where Beatrice lived, and where it must have been that she first appeared to the rapt boy who was to be the world's Dante, "clothed in a most noble color, a modest and becoming crimson, garlanded and adorned in such wise as befitted her very youthful age." The palace of the Salviati – in which Cosimo I. was born, and in which his father, Giovanni delle Bande Nere, taught the child courage by flinging him from an upper window into the arms of a servitor below – has long occupied the site of the older edifice; and the Piazza Donati, whatever dignity it may once have had, is now nothing better than a shabby court. The back windows of the tall houses surrounding it look into it when not looking into one another, and see there a butcher's shop, a smithy, a wagon-maker's, and an inn for peasants with stabling. On a day when I was there, a wash stretched fluttering across the rear of Dante's house, and the banner of a green vine trailed from a loftier balcony. From one of the Donati casements an old woman in a purple knit jacket was watching a man repainting an omnibus in front of the wagon-shop; a great number of canaries sang in cages all round the piazza; a wrinkled peasant with a faded green cotton umbrella under his arm gave the place an effect of rustic sojourn; and a diligence that two playful stable-boys were long in hitching up drove jingling out, with its horses in brass-studded head-stalls, past where I stood under the fine old arches of the gateway. I had nothing to object to all this, nor do I suppose that this last state of his old neighborhood much vexes the poet now. It was eminently picturesque, with a sort of simple cheerfulness of aspect, the walls of the houses in the little piazza being of different shades of buff, with window-shutters in light green opening back upon them from those casements where the shrieking canaries hung. The place had that tone which characterizes so many city perspectives in Italy, and especially Florence, – which makes the long stretch of Via Borgognissanti so smiling, and bathes the sweep of Lungarno in a sunny glow wholly independent of the state of the weather. As you stroll along one of these light-yellow avenues you say to yourself, "Ah, *this* is Florence!" And then suddenly you plunge into the gray-brown gloom of such a street as the Borgo degli Albizzi, with lofty palaces climbing in vain toward the sun, and frowning upon the street below with fronts of stone, rude or sculptured, but always stern and cold; and then that, too, seems the only Florence. They are in fact equally Florentine; but I suppose one expresses the stormy yet poetic life of the old commonwealth, and

the other the serene, sunny commonplace of the Lorrainese
régime.

I was not sorry to find this the tone of Piazza Donati,
into which I had eddied from the austerity of Borgo degli
Albizzi. It really belongs to a much remoter period than
the older-looking street, – to the Florence that lingers ar-
chitecturally yet in certain narrow avenues to the Mercato
Vecchio, where the vista is broken by innumerable pent-
roofs, balconies, and cornices; and a throng of operatic
figures in slouch hats and short cloaks are so very improbably bent on any realistic business, that they seem to bo
masquerading there in the mysterious fumes of the cook-
shops. Yet I should be loath, for no very tangible reason,
to have Piazza Donati like one of these avenues or in any
wise different from what it is; certainly I should not like to
have the back of Dante's house smartened up like the front,
which looks into the Piazza San Martino. I do not complain
that the restoration is bad; it is even very good, for all that I
know; but the unrestored back is better, and I have a general
feeling that the past ought to be allowed to tumble down in
peace, though I have no doubt that whenever this happened
I should be one of the first to cry out against the barbarous
indifference that suffered it. I dare say that in a few hundred year, when the fact of the restoration is forgotten, the
nineteenth-century mediævalism of Dante's house will be
acceptable to the most fastidious tourist. I tried to get into
the house, which is open to the public at certain hours on
certain days, but I always came at ten on Saturday, when
I ought to have come at two on Monday, or the like; and
so at last I had to content myself with the interior of the

little church of San Martino, where Dante was married, half
a stone's-cast from where he was born. The church was
closed, and I asked a cobbler, who had brought his work to
the threshold of his shop hard by, for the sake of the light,
where the sacristan lived. He answered me unintelligibly,
without leaving off for a moment his furious hammering at
the shoe in his lap. He must have been asked that question a
great many times, and I do not know that I should have taken
any more trouble in his place; but a woman in a fruit-stall
next door had pity on me, knowing doubtless that I was
interested in San Martino on account of the "wedding, and
sent me to No. 1. But No. 1 was a house so improbably
genteel that I had not the courage to ring; and I asked the
grocer alongside for a better direction. He did not know
how to give it, but he sent me to the local apothecary, who in
turn sent me to another number. Here another shoemaker,
friendlier or idler than the first, left off gossiping with some
friends of his, and showed me the right door at last in the rear
of the church. My pull at the bell shot the sacristan's head
out of the fourth-story window in the old way that always
delighted me, and I perceived even at that distance that he
was a man perpetually fired with zeal for his church by the
curiosity of strangers. I could certainly see the church, yes;
he would come down instantly and open it from the inside
if I would do him the grace to close his own door from
the outside. I complied willingly, and in another moment I
stood within the little temple, where, upon the whole, for
the sake of the emotion that divine genius, majestic sorrow,
and immortal fame can accumulate within one's average
commonplaceness, it is as well to stand as any other spot

on earth. It is a very little place, with one-third of the space divided from the rest by an iron-tipped wooden screen. Behind this is the simple altar, and here Dante Alighieri and Gemma Donati were married. In whatever state the walls were then, they are now plainly whitewashed, though in one of the lunettes forming a sort of frieze half round the top was a fresco said to represent the espousals of the poet. The church was continually visited, the sacristan told me, by all sorts of foreigners, English, French, Germans, Spaniards, even Americans, but especially Russians, the most impassioned of all for it. One of this nation, one Russian eminent even among his impassioned race, spent several hours in looking at that picture, taking his stand at the foot of the stairs by which the sacristan descended from his lodging into the church. He showed me the very spot; I do not know why, unless he took me for another Russian, and thought my pride in a compatriot so impassioned might have some effect upon the fee I was to give him. He was a credulous sacristan, and I cannot find any evidence in Miss Horner's faithful and trusty "Walks in Florence" that there is a fresco in that church representing the espousals of Dante. The paintings in the lunettes are by a pupil of Masaccio's, and deal with the good works of the twelve Good Men of San Martino, who, ever since 1441, have had charge of a fund for the relief of such shamefaced poor as were unwilling to ask alms. Prince Strozzi and other patricians of Florence are at present among these Good Men, so the sacristan said; and there is an iron contribution-box at the church door, with an inscription promising any giver indulgence, successively guaranteed by four popes, of twenty-four hundred years; which seemed really to make it worth one's while.

## XIV.

In visiting these scenes, one cannot but wonder at the small compass in which the chief facts of Dante's young life, suitably to the home-keeping character of the time and race, occurred. There he was born, there he was bred, and there he was married to Gemma Donati after Beatrice Portinari died. Beatrice's father lived just across the way from the Donati houses, and the Donati houses adjoined the house where Dante grew up with his widowed mother. He saw Beatrice in her father's house, and he must often have been in the house of Manetto de' Donati as a child. As a youth he no doubt made love to Gemma at her casement; and here they must have dwelt after they were married, and she began to lead him a restless and unhappy life, being a fretful and foolish woman, by the accounts.

One realizes all this there with a distinctness which the clearness of the Italian atmosphere permits. In that air events do not seem to age any more than edifices; a life, like a structure, of six hundred years ago seems of yesterday, and one feels toward the Donati as if that troublesome family were one's own contemporaries. The evil they brought on Dante was not domestic only, but they and their party were the cause of his exile and his barbarous sentence in the process of the evil times which brought the Bianchi and Neri to Florence.

There is in history hardly anything so fantastically malicious, so tortuous, so perverse, as the series of chances that ended in his banishment. Nothing could apparently have been more remote from him, to all human perception, than

that quarrel of a Pistoja family, in which the children of
Messer Cancelliere's first wife, Bianca, called themselves
Bianchi, and the children of the second called themselves
Neri, simply for contrary-mindedness' sake. But let us follow it, and see how it reaches the poet and finally delivers
him over to a life of exile and misery. One of these Cancellieri of Pistoja falls into a quarrel with another and wounds
him with his sword. They are both boys, or hardly more,
and the father of the one who struck the blow bids him go to
his kinsmen and beg their forgiveness. But when he comes
to them the father of the wounded youth takes him out to
the stable, and striking off the offending hand on a block
there, flings it into his face. "Go back to your father and tell
him that hurts are healed with iron, not with words."

The news of this cruel deed throws all Pistoja into an
incomprehensible mediæval frenzy. The citizens arm and
divide themselves into Bianchi and Neri; the streets become
battle-fields. Finally some cooler heads ask Florence to interfere. Florence is always glad to get a finger into the affairs
of her neighbors, and to quiet Pistoja she calls the worst of
the Bianchi and Neri to her. Her own factions take promptly
to the new names; the Guelphs have long ruled the city; the
Ghibellines have been a whole generation in exile. But the
Neri take up the old Ghibelline *rôle* of invoking foreign intervention, with Corso Donati at their head, – a brave man,
but hot, proud, and lawless. Dante is of the Bianchi party,
which is that of the liberals and patriots, and in this quality
he goes to Rome to plead with the Pope to use his good
offices for the peace and freedom of Florence. In his absence
he is banished for two years and heavily fined; then he is

banished for life, and will be burned if he comes back. His party comes into power, but the sentence is never repealed, and in the despair of exile Dante, too, invokes the stranger's help. He becomes Nero; he dies Ghibelline.

I walked up from the other Donati houses through the Via Borgo degli Albizzi to the Piazza San Pier Maggiore to look at the truncated tower of Corso Donati, in which he made his last stand against the people when summoned by their Podestà to answer for all his treasons and seditions. He fortified the adjoining houses, and embattled the whole neighborhood, galling his besiegers in the streets below with showers of stones and arrows. They set fire to his fortress, and then he escaped through the city wall into the open country, but was hunted down and taken by his enemies. On the way back to Florence he flung himself from his horse, that they might not have the pleasure of triumphing with him through the streets, and the soldier in charge of him was surprised into running him through with his lance, as Corso intended. This is the story that some tell; but others say that his horse ran away, dragging him over the road by his foot, which caught in his stirrup, and the guard killed him, seeing him already hurt to death. Dante favors the latter version of his end, and sees him in hell, torn along at the heels of a beast, whose ceaseless flight is toward "the valley where never mercy is."

The poet had once been the friend as well as brother-in-law of Corso, but had turned against him when Corso's lust of power threatened the liberties of Florence. You must see this little space of the city to understand how intensely narrow and local the great poet was in his hates and loves, and how considerably he has populated hell and purgatory with his old neighbors and acquaintance. Among those whom he puts in Paradise was that sister of Corso's, the poor Piccarda, whose story is one of the most pathetic and pious legends of that terrible old Florence. The vain and worldly life which she saw around her had turned her thoughts toward heaven, and she took the veil in the convent of Santa Chiara. Her brother was then at Bologna, but he repaired straightway to Florence with certain of his followers, forced the convent, and dragging his sister forth amid the cries and prayers of the nuns, gave her to wife to Rosellino della Tosa, a gentleman to whom he had promised her. She, in the bridal garments with which he had replaced her nun's robes, fell on her knees and implored the succor of her Heavenly Spouse, and suddenly her beautiful body was covered with a loathsome leprosy, and in a few days she died inviolate. Some will have it that she merely fell into a slow infirmity, and so pined away. Corso Donati was the brother of Dante's wife, and without ascribing to Gemma more of his quality than Piccarda's, one may readily perceive that the poet had not married into a comfortable family.

In the stump of the old tower which I had come to see, I found a poulterer's shop, bloody and evil-smelling, and two frowzy girls picking chickens. In the wall there is a tablet signed by the Messer Capitani of the Guelph Party, forbidding any huckster to sell his wares in that square under pain of a certain fine. The place now naturally abounds in them.

The Messer Capitani are all dead, with their party, and the hucksters are no longer afraid.

## XV.

Or my part, I find it hard to be serious about the tragedy of a people who seem, as me looks back at them in their history, to have lived in such perpetual broil as the Florentines. They cease to be even pathetic; they become absurd, and tempt the observer to a certain mood of triviality, by their indefatigable antics in cutting and thrusting, chopping off heads, mutilating, burning, and banishing. But I have often thought that we must get a false impression of the past by the laws governing perspective, in which the remoter objects are inevitably pressed together in their succession, and the spaces between are ignored. In looking at a painting, these spaces are imagined; but in history, the objects, the events are what alone make their appeal, and there seems nothing else. It must always remain for the reader to revise his impressions, and rearrange them, so as to give some value to conditions as well as to occurrences. It looks very much, at first glance, as if the Florentines bad no peace from the domination of the Romans to the domination of the Medici. But in all that time they had been growing in wealth, power, the arts and letters, and were constantly striving to realize in their state the ideal which is still our only political aim — "a government of the people by the people for the people." Whoever opposed himself, his interests or his pride, to that ideal, was destroyed sooner or later; and it appears that if there had been no foreign interference, the one-man power would never have been fastened on Florence. We must account, therefore, not only for seasons of repose not obvious in history, but for a measure of success in the realization of her political ideal. The feudal nobles, forced into the city from their petty sovereignties beyond its gates; the rich merchants and bankers, creators and creatures of its prosperity; the industrious and powerful guilds of artisans; the populace of unskilled laborers, — authority visited each in turn; but no class could long keep it from the others, and no man from all the rest. The fluctuations were violent enough, but they only seem incessant through the necessities of perspective; and somehow, in the most turbulent period, there was peace enough for the industries to fruit and the arts to flower. Now and then a whole generation passed in which there was no upheaval, though it must be owned that these generations seem few. A life of the ordinary compass witnessed so many atrocious scenes, that Dante, who peopled his Inferno with his neighbors and fellow-citizens, had but to study their manners and customs to give life to his picture. Forty years after his exile, when the Florentines rose to drive out Walter of Brienne, the Duke of Athens, whom they had made their ruler, and who had tried to make himself their master by a series of cruel oppressions, they stormed the Palazzo Vecchio, where he had taken refuge, and demanded certain of his bloody minions; and when his soldiers thrust one of these out among them, they cut him into small pieces, and some tore the quivering fragments with their teeth.

## XVI.

The savage lurks so near the surface in every man that a constant watch must be kept upon the passions and impulses, or he leaps out in his war-paint, and the poor integument of civilization that held him is flung aside like a useless garment. The Florentines were a race of impulse and passion, and the mob was merely the frenzy of that popular assemblage by which the popular will made itself known, the suffrage being a thing as yet imperfectly understood and only secondarily exercised. Yet the peacefulest and apparently the wholesomest time known to the historians was that which followed the expulsion of the Duke of Athens, when the popular mob, having defeated the aristocratic leaders of the revolt, came into power, with such unquestionable authority that the nobles were debarred from office, and punished not only in their own persons, but in kith and kin, for offences against the life of a plebeian. Five hundred noble families were exiled, and of those left, the greater part sued to be admitted among the people. This grace was granted them, but upon the condition that they must not aspire to office for five years, and that if any of them killed or grievously wounded a plebeian, he should be immediately and hopelessly re-ennobled; which sounds like some fantastic invention of Mr. Frank R. Stockton's, and only too vividly recalls *Lord Tolloller's* appeal in "Iolanthe:"

> "Spurn not the nobly born
> With love affected,
> Nor treat with virtuous scorn
> The well-connected.
> High rank involves no shame
> We boast an equal claim
> With him of humble name
> To be respected."

The world has been ruled so long by the most idle and worthless people in it, that it always seems droll to see those who earn the money spending it, and those from whom the power comes using it. But we who are now trying to offer this ridiculous spectacle to the world ought not to laugh at it in the Florentine government of 1343–46. It seems to have lasted no long time, for at the end of three or four years the divine wrath smote Florence with the pest. This was to chastise her for her sins, as the chroniclers tell us; but as a means of reform it failed apparently. A hundred thousand of the people died, and the rest, demoralized by the terror and enforced idleness in which they had lived, abandoned themselves to all manner of dissolute pleasures, and were much worse than if they had never had any pest. This pest, of which the reader will find a lively account in Boccaccio's introduction to the "Decamerone," – he was able to write of it because, like De Foe, who described the plague of London, he had not seen it, – seems rather to have been a blow at popular government, if we may judge from the disorders which it threw the democratic city into, and the long train of wars and miseries that presently followed. But few of us are ever sufficiently in the divine confidence to be able to say just why this or that thing happens, and we are constantly growing more modest about assuming to know. What is certain is that the one-man power, foreboded and resisted from the first in Florence, was at last to possess itself of the fierce and jealous city. It showed itself, of course, in a patriotic and beneficent aspect at the beginning, but within a generation the first memorable Medici had befriended the popular cause and had made the weight of his name felt in Florence. From Salvestro de' Medici, who succeeded in breaking the power of the Guelph nobles in 1382, and, however unwillingly, promoted the Tumult of the Ciompi and the rule of the lowest classes, it is a long step to Averardo de' Medici, another popular leader in 1421; and it is again another long step from him to Cosimo de' Medici, who got himself called the Father of his Country, and died in 1469, leaving her with her throat fast in the clutch of his nephew, Lorenzo the Magnificent. But it was the stride of destiny, and nothing apparently could stay it.

## XVII.

The name of Lorenzo de' Medici is the next name of un-rivalled greatness to which one comes in Florence after Dante's. The Medici, however one may be principled against them, do possess the imagination there, and I could not have helped going for their sake to the Piazza of the Mercato Vec-chio, even if I had not wished to see again and again one of the most picturesque and characteristic places in the city. As I think of it, the pale, delicate sky of a fair winters day in Florence spreads over me, and I seem to stand in the midst of the old square, with its mouldering colonnade on one side, and on the other its low, irregular roofs, their brown tiles thinly tinted with a growth of spindling grass and weeds, green the whole year round. In front of me a vast, white old palace springs seven stories into the sunshine, disreputably shabby from basement to attic, but beautiful, with the rags of a plebeian wash-day caught across it from balcony to balcony, as if it had fancied trying to hide its forlornness in them. Around me are peasants and donkey-carts and Florentines of all sizes and ages; my ears are filled with the sharp din of an Italian crowd, and my nose with the smell of immemorial, innumerable market-days, and the rank, cutting savor of frying fish and cakes from a score of neighboring cook-shops; but I am happy, — happier than I should probably be if I were actually there. Through an archway in the street behind me, not far from an admirably tumble-down shop full of bricabrac of low degree, all huddled — old bureaus and bedsteads, crockery, classic lamps, assorted saints, shovels, flat-irons, and big-eyed madonnas — under a sagging pent-roof, I enter a large court, like Piazza Donati. Here the Medici, among other great citizens, had their first houses; and in the narrow street opening out of this court stands the little church which was then the family chapel of the Medici, after the fashion of that time, where all their marriages, christenings, and funerals took place. In time this highly respectable quarter suffered the sort of social decay which so frequently and so capriciously affects highly respectable quarters in all cities; and it had at last fallen so low, in the reign of Cosimo I, that when that grim tyrant wished cheaply to please the Florentines by making it a little harder for the Jews than for the Christians under him, he shut them up in the old court. They had been let into Florence to counteract the extortion of the Christian usurers, and upon the condition that they would not ask more than twenty per cent interest. How much more had been taken by the Christians one can hardly imagine; but if this was a low rate to Florentines, one easily understands how the bankers of the city grew rich by lending to the necessitous world outside. Now and then they did not get back their principal, and Edward III of England has still an outstanding debt to the house of Peruzzi, which he bankrupted in the fourteenth century. The best of the Jews left the city rather than enter the Ghetto, and only the baser sort remained to its captivity. Whether any of them still continue there, I do not know; but the place has grown more and more disreputable, till now it is the home of the forlornest rabble I saw in Florence, and if they were not the worst, their looks are unjust to them. They were mainly women and children, as the worst classes seem to be everywhere, – I do not know why, – and the air was full of the clatter of their feet and tongues, intolerably reverberated from the high many-windowed walls of scorbutic brick and stucco. These walls were, of course, garlanded with garments hung to dry from their casements. It is perpetually washing-day in Italy, and the observer, seeing so much linen washed and so little clean, is everywhere invited to the solution of one of the strangest problems of the Latin civilization.

The ancient home of the Medici has none of the feudal dignity, the baronial pride, of the quarter of the Lamberti and the Buondelmonti; and, disliking them as I did, I was glad to see it in the possession of that squalor, so different from the cheerful and industrious thrift of Piazza Donati and the neighborhood of Dante's house. No touch of sympathetic poetry relieves the history of that race of demagogues and tyrants, who, in their rise, had no thought but to aggrandize themselves, and whose only greatness was an apotheosis of egotism. It is hard to understand through what law of development, from lower to higher, the Providence which rules the affairs of men permitted them supremacy; and it is easy to understand how the better men whom they supplanted and dominated should abhor them. They were especially a bitter dose to the proud-stomached aristocracy of citizens which had succeeded the extinct Ghibelline nobility in Florence; but, indeed, the three pills which they adopted from the arms of their guild of physicians, together with the only appellation by which history knows their lineage, were agreeable to none who wished their country well. From the first Medici to the last, they were nearly all hypocrites or ruffians, bigots or imbeciles; and Lorenzo, who was a scholar and a poet, and the friend of scholars and poets, had the genius and science of tyranny in supreme degree, though he wore no princely title and assumed to be only the chosen head of the commonwealth.

"Under his rule," says Villari, in his "Life of Savonarola," that almost incomparable biography, "all wore a prosperous and contented aspect; the parties that had so long disquieted the city were at peace; imprisoned, or banished, or dead, those who would not submit to the Medicean domination; tranquillity and calm were everywhere. Feasting, dancing, public shows, and games amused the Florentine people, who, once so jealous of their rights, seemed to have forgotten even the name of liberty. Lorenzo, who took part in all these pleasures, invented new ones every day. But among all his inventions, the most famous was that of the carnival songs (*canti carnascialeschi*), of which he composed the first, and which were meant to be sung in the masquerades of carnival, when the youthful nobility, disguised to represent the Triumph of Death, or a crew of demons, or some other caprice of fancy, wandered through the city, filling it with their riot. The reading of these songs will paint the corruption of the town far better than any other description. To-day, not only the youthful nobility, but the basest of the populace, would hold them in loathing, and to go singing them through the city would be an offence to public decency which could not fail to be punished. These things were the favorite recreation of a prince lauded by all the world and held up as a model to every sovereign, a prodigy of wisdom, a political and literary genius. And such as they called him then, many would judge him still," says our author, who explicitly warns his readers against Roscoe's "Life of Lorenzo de' Medici," as the least trustworthy of all in its characterization. "They would forgive him the blood spilt to maintain a dominion unjustly acquired by him and his; the disorder wrought in the commonwealth; the theft of the public treasure to supply his profligate waste; the shameless vices to which in spite of his feeble health he abandoned himself; and even that rapid and infernal corruption of the people, which he perpetually studied with all the force and capacity of his soul." And all because he was the protector of letters and the fine arts!

"In the social condition of Florence at that time there was indeed a strange contrast. Culture was universally diffused; everybody knew Latin and Greek, everybody admired the classics; many ladies were noted for the elegance of their Greek and Latin verses. The arts, which had languished since the time of Giotto, revived, and on all sides rose exquisite palaces and churches. But artists, scholars, politicians, nobles, and plebeians were rotten at heart, lacking in every public and private virtue, every moral sentiment. Religion was the tool of the government or vile hypocrisy; they had neither civil, nor religious, nor moral, nor philosophic faith; even doubt feebly asserted itself in their souls. A cold indifference to every principle prevailed, and those visages full of guile and subtlety wore a smile of chilly superiority and compassion at any sign of enthusiasm for noble and generous ideas. They did not oppose these or question them, as a philosophical sceptic would have done; they simply pitied them. . . . But Lorenzo had an exquisite taste for poetry and the arts. . . . Having set himself up to protect artists and scholars, his house became the resort of the most illustrious wits of his time, . . . and whether in the meetings under his own roof, or in those of the famous Platonic Academy, his own genius shone brilliantly in that elect circle. . . . A strange life indeed was Lorenzo's. After giving his whole mind and soul to the destruction, by some new law, of some last remnant of liberty, after pronouncing some fresh sentence of ruin or death, he entered the Platonic Academy, and ardently discussed virtue and the immortality of the soul; then sallying forth to mingle with the dissolute youth of the city, he sang his carnival songs, and abandoned himself to debauchery; returning home with Pulci and Politian, he recited verses and talked of poetry; and to each of these occupations he gave himself up as wholly as if it were the sole occupation of his life. But the strangest thing of all is that in all that variety of life they cannot cite a solitary act of real generosity toward his people, his friends, or his kinsmen; for surely if there had been such an act, his indefatigable flatterers would not have forgotten it. . . . He had inherited from Cosimo all that subtlety by which, without being a great statesman, he was prompt in cunning subterfuges, full of prudence and acuteness, skilful in dealing with ambassadors, most skilful in extinguishing his enemies, bold and cruel when he believed the occasion permitted. . . . His face revealed his character; there was something sinister and hateful in it; the complexion was greenish, the mouth very large, the nose flat, and the voice nasal; but his eye was quick and keen, his forehead was high, and his manner had all of gentleness that can be imagined of an age so refined and elegant as that; his conversation was full of vivacity, of wit and learning; those who were admitted to his familiarity were always fascinated by him. He seconded his age in all its tendencies; corrupt as it was, he left it corrupter still in every way; he gave himself up to pleasure, and he taught his people to give themselves up to it, to its intoxication and its delirium."

## XVIII.

This is the sort of being whom human nature in self-defence ought always to recognize as a devil, and whom no glamour of circumstance or quality should be suffered to disguise. It is success like his which, as Victor Hugo says of Louis Napoleon's similar success, "confounds the human conscience," and kindles the lurid light in which assassination seems a holy duty. Lorenzo's tyranny in Florence was not only the extinction of public liberty, but the control of private life in all its relations. He made this marriage and he forbade that among the principal families, as it suited his pleasure; he decided employments and careers; he regulated the most intimate affairs of households in the interest of his power, with a final impunity which is inconceivable of that proud and fiery Florence. The smoldering resentment of his tyranny, which flamed out in the conspiracy of the Pazzi, adds the consecration of a desperate love of liberty to the cathedral, hallowed by religion and history, in which the tragedy was enacted. It was always dramatizing itself there when I entered the Duomo, whether in the hush and twilight of some vacant hour, or in the flare of

tapers and voices while some high ceremonial filled the vast
nave with its glittering procession. But I think the ghosts
preferred the latter setting. To tell the truth, the Duomo
at Florence is a temple to damp the spirit, dead or alive, by
the immense impression of stony bareness, of drab vacuity,
which one receives from its interior, unless it is filled with
people. Outside it is magnificently imposing, in spite of the
insufficiency and irregularity of its piazza. In spite of having
no such approach as St. Mark's at Venice, or St. Peter's
at Rome, or even the cathedral at Milan, in spite of being
almost crowded upon by the surrounding shops and cafés,
it is noble, and more and more astonishing; and there is the
baptistery, with its heavenly gates, and the tower of Giotto,
with its immortal beauty, as novel for each new-comer as
if freshly set out there overnight for his advantage. Nor do
I object at all to the cabstands there, and the little shops
all round, and the people thronging through the piazza, in
and out of the half-score of crooked streets opening upon
it. You do not get all the grandeur of the cathedral outside,
but you get enough, while you come away from the interior
in a sort of destitution. One needs some such function as
I saw there one evening at dusk in order to realize all the
spectacular capabilities of the place. This function consisted
mainly of a visible array of the Church's forces "against blas-
phemy," as the printed notices informed me; but with the
high altar blazing, a constellation of candles in the distant
gloom, and the long train of priests, choristers, acolytes,
and white-cowled penitents, each with his taper, and the
archbishop, bearing the pyx, at their head, under a silken
canopy, it formed a setting of incomparable vividness for
the scene on the last Sunday before Ascension, 1478.

There is, to my thinking, no such mirror of the spirit of that time as the story of this conspiracy. A pope was at the head of it, and an archbishop was there in Florence to share actively in it. Having failed to find Lorenzo and Giuliano de' Medici together at Lorenzo's villa, the conspirators transfer the scene to the cathedral; the moment chosen for striking the blow is that supremely sacred moment when the very body of Christ is elevated for the adoration of the kneeling worshippers. What a contempt they all have for the place and the office! In this you read one effect of that study of antiquity which was among the means Lorenzo used to corrupt the souls of men; the Florentines are half repaganized. Yet at the bottom of the heart of one conspirator lingers a mediæval compunction, and though not unwilling to kill a man, this soldier does not know about killing one in a church. Very well, then, give up your dagger, you simple soldier; give it to this priest; *he* knows what a church is, and how little sacred!

The cathedral is packed with people, and Lorenzo is there, but Giuliano is not come yet. Are we to be fooled a second time? Malediction! Send some one to fetch that Medicean beast, who is so slow coming to the slaughter! I am of the conspiracy, for I hate the Medici; but these muttered blasphemies, hissed and ground through the teeth, this frenzy for murder, – it is getting to be little better than that, – make me sick. Two of us go for Giuliano to his house, and being acquaintances of his, we laugh and joke familiarly with him; we put our arms caressingly about him, and feel if he has a shirt of mail on, as we walk him between us through the crowd at the corner of the café there, invisibly, past all the cabmen ranked near the cathedral and the baptistery,

not one of whom shall snatch his horse's oat-bag from his
nose to invite us phantoms to a turn in the city. We have
our friend safe in the cathedral at last, — hapless, kindly
youth, whom we have nothing against except that he is of
that cursed race of the Medici, — and now at last the priest
elevates the host and it is time to strike; the little bell tin-
kles, the multitude holds its breath and falls upon its knees;
Lorenzo and Giuliano kneel with the rest. A moment, and
Bernardo Bandini plunges his short dagger through the boy,
who drops dead upon his face, and Francesco Pazzi flings
himself upon the body, and blindly striking to make sure
of his death, gives himself a wound in the leg that disables
him for the rest of the work. And now we see the folly of
intrusting Lorenzo to the unpractised hand of a priest, who
would have been neat enough, no doubt, at mixing a dose
of poison. The bungler has only cut his man a little in the
neck! Lorenzo's sword is out and making desperate play for
his life; his friends close about him, and while the sacred
vessels are tumbled from the altar and trampled under foot
in the mellay, and the cathedral rings with yells and shrieks
and curses and the clash of weapons, they have hurried him
into the sacristy and barred the doors, against which we
shall beat ourselves in vain. Fury! Infamy! Malediction! Pick
yourself up, Francesco Pazzi, and get home as you may!
There is no mounting to horse and crying liberty through
the streets for you! All is over! The wretched populace, the
servile signory, side with the Medici; in a few hours the
Archbishop of Pisa is swinging by the neck from a window
of the Palazzo Vecchio; and while he is yet alive you are
dragged, bleeding and naked, from your bed through the
streets and hung beside him, so close that in his dying agony

he sets his teeth in your breast with a convulsive frenzy that leaves you fast in the death-clutch of his jaws till they cut the ropes and you ruin hideously down to the pavement below.

## XIX.

One must face these grisly details from time to time if he would feel what Florence was. All the world was like Florence at that time in its bloody cruelty; the wonder is that Florence, being what she otherwise was, should be like all the world in that. One should take the trouble also to keep constantly in mind the smallness of the theatre in which these scenes were enacted. Compared with modern cities, Florence was but a large town, and these Pazzi were neighbors and kinsmen of the Medici, and they and their fathers had seen the time when the Medici were no more in the state than other families which had perhaps scorned to rise by their arts. It would be insufferable to any of us if some acquaintance whom we knew so well, root and branch, should come to reign over us; but this is what happened through the Medici in Florence.

I walked out one pleasant Sunday afternoon to the Villa Careggi, where Lorenzo made a dramatic end twenty years after the tragedy in the cathedral. It is some two miles from the city; I could not say in just what direction; but it does not matter, since if you do not come to Villa Careggi when you go to look for it, you come to something else equally memorable, by ways as beautiful and through landscapes as picturesque. I remember that there was hanging from a crevice of one of the stone walls which we sauntered be-tween, one of those great purple anemones of Florence, tilting and swaying in the sunny air of February, and that there was a tender presentiment of spring in the atmosphere, and people were out languidly enjoying the warmth about their doors, as if the winter had been some malady of theirs, and they were now slowly convalescent. The mountains were white with snow beyond Fiesole, but that was perhaps to set off to better advantage the nearer hill-sides, studded with villas gleaming white through black plumes of cypress, and blurred with long gray stretches of olive orchard; it is impossible to escape some such crazy impression of intention in the spectacular prospect of Italy, though that is probably less the fault of the prospect than of the people who have painted and printed so much about it. There were vineyards, of course, as well as olive orchards on all those broken and irregular slopes, over which wandered a tangle of the high walls which everywhere shut you out from intimate approach to the fields about Florence; you may look up at them, afar off, or you may look down at them, but you cannot look into them on the same level.

We entered the Villa Careggi, when we got to it, through a high, grated gateway, and then we found ourselves in a delicious garden, the exquisite thrill of whose loveliness lingers yet in my utterly satisfied senses. I remember it as chiefly a plantation of rare trees, with an enchanting glimmer of the inexhaustibly various landscape through every break in their foliage; but near the house was a formal parterre for flowers, silent, serene, aristocratic, touched not with decay, but a sort of pensive regret. On a terrace yet nearer were some *putti*, some frolic boys cut in marble, with a growth of brown moss on their soft backs, and looking as if, in their lapse from the civilization for which they were designed, they had begun to clothe themselves in skins.

As to the interior of the villa, every one may go there and observe its facts; its vast, cold, dim saloons, its floors of polished cement, like ice to the foot, and its walls covered with painted histories and anecdotes and portraits of the Medici. The outside warmth had not got into the house, and I shivered in the sepulchral gloom, and could get no sense of the gay, voluptuous, living past there, not even in the prettily painted loggia where Lorenzo used to sit with his friends overlooking Val d'Arno, and glimpsing the tower of Giotto and the dome of Brunelleschi. But there is one room, next to the last of the long suite fronting on the lovely garden, where the event which makes the place memorable has an incomparable actuality. It is the room where Lorenzo died, and his dying eyes could look from its windows out over the lovely garden, and across the vast stretches of villa and village, olive and cypress, to the tops of Florence swimming against the horizon. He was a long time dying, of the gout of his ancestors and his own debauchery, and he drew near his end cheerfully enough, and very much as he had always lived, now reasoning high of philosophy and poetry with Pico della Mirandola and Politian, and now laughing at the pranks of the jesters and buffoons whom they brought in to amuse him, till the very last, when he sickened of all those delights, fine or gross, and turned his thoughts to the mercy despised so long. But, as he kept saying, none had ever dared give him a resolute No, save one; and dreading in his final hours the mockery of flattering priests, he sent for this one fearless soul; and Savonarola, who had never yielded to his threats or caresses, came at the prayer of the dying man, and took his place beside the bed we still see there, – high, broad, richly carved in dark wood, with a picture of Perugino's on the wall at the left beside it. Piero, Lorenzo's son, from whom he has just parted, must be in the next room yet, and the gentle Pico della Mirandola, whom Lorenzo was so glad to see that he smiled and jested with him in the old way, has closed the door on the preacher and the sinner. Lorenzo confesses that he has heavy on his soul three crimes: the cruel sack of Volterra, the theft of the public dower of young girls, by which many were driven to a wicked life, and the blood shed after the conspiracy of the Pazzi. "He was greatly agitated, and Savonarola to quiet him kept repeating 'God is good; God is merciful. But,' he added, when Lorenzo had ceased to speak, 'there is need of three things.' 'And what are they, father?' 'First, you must have a great and living faith in the mercy of God.' 'This I have – the greatest.' 'Second, you must restore that which you have wrongfully taken, or require your children to restore it for you.' Lorenzo looked surprised and troubled; but he forced himself to compliance, and nodded his head in sign of assent. Then Savonarola rose to his feet, and stood over the dying prince. 'Last, you must give back their liberty to the people of Florence.' Lorenzo, summoning all his remaining strength, disdainfully turned his back; and, without uttering a word, Savonarola departed without giving him absolution."

It was as if I saw and heard it all, as I stood there in the room where the scene had been enacted; it still remains to me the vividest event in Florentine history, and Villari has no need, for me at least, to summon all the witnesses he calls to establish the verity of the story. There are some disputed things that establish themselves in our credence through the nature of the men and the times of which they are told, and this is one of them. Lorenzo and Savonarola were equally matched in courage, and the Italian soul of the one was as subtle for good as the Italian soul of the other was subtle for evil. In that encounter, the preacher knew that it was not the sack of a city or the blood of conspirators for which the sinner really desired absolution, however artfully and naturally they were advanced in his appeal; and Lorenzo knew when he sent for him that the monk would touch the sore spot in his guilty heart unerringly. It was a profound drama, searching the depths of character on either side, and on either side it was played with matchless magnanimity.

## XX.

After I had been at Careggi, I had to go again and look at San Marco, at the cell to which Savonarola returned from that death-bed, sorrowing. Yet, at this distance of time and place, one must needs wonder a little why one is so pitiless to Lorenzo, so devoted to Savonarola. I have a suspicion, which I own with shame and reluctance, that I should have liked Lorenzo's company much better, and that I, too, should have felt to its last sweetness the charm of his manner. I confess that I think I should have been bored – it is well to be honest with one's self in all things – by the menaces and mystery of Savonarola's prophesying, and that I should have thought his crusade against the pomps and vanities of Florence a vulgar and ridiculous business. He and his monks would have been terribly dull companions for one of my make within their convent; and when they came out and danced in a ring with his male and female devotees in the square before the church, I should have liked them no better than so many soldiers of the Army of Salvation. That is not my idea of the way in which the souls of men are to be purified and elevated, or their thoughts turned to God. Puerility and vulgarity of a sort to set one's teeth on edge marked the excesses which Savonarola permitted in his followers; and if he could have realized his puritanic republic, it would have been one of the heaviest yokes about the neck of poor human nature that have ever burdened it. For the reality would have been totally different from the ideal. So far as we can understand, the popular conception of Savonarola's doctrine was something as gross as Army-of-Salvationism, as wild and sensuous as backwoods Wesleyism, as fantastic, as spiritually arrogant as primitive Quakerism, as bleak and grim as militant Puritanism. We must face these facts, and the fact that Savonarola, though a Puritan, was no Protestant at all, but the most devout of Catholics, even while he defied the Pope. He was a sublime and eloquent preacher, a genius inspired to ecstasy with the beauty of holiness; but perhaps – perhaps! – Lorenzo knew the Florentines better than he when he turned his face away and died unshriven rather than give them back their freedom. Then why, now that they have both been dust for four hundred years, – and in all things the change is such that if not a new heaven there is a new earth since their day, – why do we cling tenderly, devoutly, to the strange, frenzied apostle of the Impossible, and turn, abhorring, from that gay, accomplished, charming, wise, and erudite statesman who knew what men were so much better? There is nothing of Savonarola now but the memory of his purpose, nothing of Lorenzo but the memory of his;

and now we see, far more clearly than if the *frate* had founded
his free state upon the ruins of the *magnifico's* tyranny, that
the one willed only good to others, and the other willed
it only to himself. All history, like each little individual
experience, enforces nothing but this lesson of altruism;
and it is because the memory which consecrates the church
of San Marco teaches it in supreme degree that one stands
before it with a swelling heart.

In itself the church is nowise interesting or imposing,
with that ugly and senseless classicism of its façade, which
associates itself with Spain rather than Italy, and the stretch
of its plain, low convent walls. It looks South American, it
looks Mexican, with its plaza-like piazza; and the alien effect
is heightened by the stiff tropical plants set round the recent
military statue in the centre. But when you are within the
convent gate, all is Italian, all is Florentine again; for there is
nothing more Florentine in Florence than those old convent
courts into which your sight-seeing takes you so often. The
middle space is enclosed by the sheltering cloisters, and here
the grass lies green in the sun the whole winter through,
with daisies in it, and other simple little sympathetic weeds
or flowers; the still air is warm, and the place has a climate
of its own. Of course, the Dominican friars are long gone
from San Marco; the place is a museum now, admirably
kept up by the Government. I paid a franc to go in, and
found the old cloister so little conventual that there was
a pretty girl copying a fresco in one of the lunettes, who
presently left her scaldino on her scaffolding, and got down
to start the blood in her feet by a swift little promenade
under the arches where the monks used to walk, and over
the dead whose gravestones pave the way. You cannot help

those things; and she was really very pretty, – much prettier than a monk. In one of the cells upstairs there was another young lady; she was copying a Fra Angelico, who might have been less shocked at her presence than some would think. He put a great number of women, as beautiful as he could paint them, in the frescos with which he has illuminated the long line of cells. In one place he has left his own portrait in a saintly company, looking on at an Annunciation: a very handsome youth, with an air expressive of an artistic rather than a spiritual interest in the fact represented, which indeed has the effect merely of a polite interview. One looks at the frescos glimmering through the dusk of the little rooms in hardly discernible detail, with more or less care, according to one's real or attempted delight in them, and then suddenly comes to the cell of Savonarola; and all the life goes out of those remote histories and allegories, and pulses in an agony of baffled good in this martyrdom. Here is the desk at which he read and wrote; here are laid some leaves of his manuscript, as if they had just trembled from those wasted hands of his; here is the hair shirt he wore, to mortify and torment that suffering flesh the more; here is a bit of charred wood gathered from the fire in which he expiated his love for the Florentines by a hideous death at their hands. It rends the heart to look at them! Still, after four hundred years, the event is as fresh as yesterday, – as fresh as Calvary; and never can the race which still gropes blindly here conceive of its divine source better than in the sacrifice of some poor fellow-creature who perishes by those to whom he meant nothing but good.

As one stands in the presence of these pathetic witnesses, the whole lamentable tragedy rehearses itself again, with

a power that makes one an actor in it. Here, I am of that
Florence which has sprung erect after shaking the foot of
the tyrant from its neck, too fiercely free to endure the
yoke of the reformer; and I perceive the waning strength
of Savonarola's friends, the growing number of his foes. I
stand with the rest before the Palazzo Vecchio waiting for
the result of that ordeal by fire to which they have challenged
his monks in test of his claims, and I hear with foreboding
the murmurs of the crowd when they are balked of their
spectacle by that question between the Dominicans and the
Franciscans about carrying the host through the flames; I return with him heavy and sorrowful to his convent, prescient
of broken power over the souls which his voice has swayed
so long; I am there in San Marco when he rises to preach,
and the gathering storm of insult and outrage bursts upon
him, with hisses and yells, till the battle begins between his
Piagnoni and the Arrabbiati, and rages through the consecrated edifice, and that fiery Peter among his friars beats in
the skulls of his assailants with the bronze crucifix caught up
from the altar; I am in the piazza before the church when
the mob attacks the convent, and the monks, shaking off his
meek control, reply with musket-shots from their cells; I
am with him when the signory sends to lead him a prisoner
to the Bargello; I am there when they stretch upon the rack
that frail and delicate body, which fastings and vigils and the
cloistered life have wrought up to a nervous sensibility as
keen as woman's; I hear his confused and uncertain replies
under the torture when they ask him whether he claims now
to have prophesied from God; I climb with him, for that
month's respite they allow him before they put him to the
question again, to the narrow cell high up in the tower of

the Old Palace, where, with the roofs and towers of the cruel city he had so loved far below him, and the purple hills misty against the snow-clad mountains all round the horizon, he recovers something of his peace of mind, and keeps his serenity of soul; I follow him down to the chapel beautiful with Ghirlandajo's frescos, where he spends his last hours, before they lead him between the two monks who are to suffer with him; and once more I stand among the pitiless multitude in the piazza. They make him taste the agony of death twice in the death of his monks; then he submits his neck to the halter and the hangman thrusts him from the scaffold, where the others hang dangling in their chains above the pyre that is to consume their bodies. "Prophet!" cries an echo of the mocking voice on Calvary, "now is the time for a miracle!" The hangman thinks to please the crowd by playing the buffoon with the quivering form; a yell of abhorrence breaks from them, and he makes haste to descend and kindle the fire that it may reach Savonarola while he is still alive. A wind rises and blows the flame away. The crowd shrinks back terrified: "A miracle! a miracle!" But the wind falls again, and the bodies slowly burn, dropping a rain of blood into the hissing embers. The heat moving the right hand of Savonarola, he seems to lift it and bless the multitude. The Piagnoni fall sobbing and groaning to their knees; the Arrabbiati set on a crew of ribald boys, who, dancing and yelling round the fire, pelt the dead martyrs with a shower of stones.

Once more I was in San Marco, but it was now in the nineteenth century, on a Sunday of January, 1883. There, in the place of Savonarola, who, though surely no Protestant, was one of the precursors of the Reformation, stood a

Northern priest, chief perhaps of those who would lead us back to Rome, appealing to us in the harsh sibilants of our English, where the Dominican had rolled the organ harmonies of his impassioned Italian upon his hearers' souls. I have certainly nothing to say against Monsignor Capel, and I have never seen a more picturesque figure than his as he stood in his episcopal purple against the curtain of pale green behind him, his square priest's cap on his fine head, and the embroidered sleeves of some ecclesiastical under-vestment showing at every tasteful gesture. His face was strong, and beautiful with its deep-sunk dreamy eyes, and he preached with singular vigor and point to a congregation of all the fashionable and cultivated English-speaking people in Florence, and to larger numbers of Italians whom I suspected of coming partly to improve themselves in our tongue. They could not have done better; his English was exquisite in diction and accent, and his matter was very good. He was warning us against Agnosticism and the limitations of merely scientific wisdom; but I thought that there was little need to persuade us of God in a church where Savonarola had lived and aspired; and that even the dead, who had known him and heard him, and who now sent up their chill through the pavement from the tombs below, and made my feet so very cold, were more eloquent of immortality in that place.

## XXI.

One morning, early in February, I walked ont through the picturesqueness of Oltrarno, and up the long ascent of the street to Porta San Giorgio, for the purpose of revering what is left of the fortifications designed by Michael Angelo

for the defence of the city in the great siege of 1535. There
are many things to distract even the most resolute pilgrim
on the way to that gate, and I was but too willing to loiter.
There are bricabrac shops on the Ponte Vecchio, and in the
Via Guicciardini and the Piazza Pitti, with old canvases, and
carvings, and bronzes in their windows; and though a little
past the time of life when one piously looks up the scenes
of fiction, I had to make an excursion up the Vin de' Bardi
for the sake of Romola, whose history begins in that street.
It is a book which you must read again in Florence, for it
gives a true and powerful impression of Savonarola's time,
even if the author does burden her drama and dialogue with
too much history. The Via de' Bardi, moreover, is worthy a
visit for its own Gothic-palaced, mediæval sake, and for the
sake of that long stretch of the Boboli garden wall backing
upon it with ivy flung over its shoulder, and a murmur
of bees in some sort of invisible blossoms beyond. In that
neighborhood I had to stop a moment before the house –
simple, but keeping its countenance in the presence of a
long line of Guicciardini palaces – where Machiavelli lived;
a barber has his shop on the ground floor now, and not
far off, again, are the houses of the Canigiani, the maternal
ancestors of Petrarch. And yet a little way, up a steep,
winding street, is the house of Galileo. It bears on its front a
tablet recording the great fact that Ferdinand II. de' Medici
visited his valued astronomer there, and a portrait of the
astronomer is painted on the stucco; there is a fruiterer
underneath, and there are a great many children playing
about, and their mothers screaming at them. The vast sky
is blue without a speck overhead, and I look down on the
tops of garden trees, and the brown-tiled roofs of houses

sinking in ever richer and softer picturesqueness from level to level below. But to get the prospect in all its wonderful beauty, one must push on up the street a little farther, and pass out between two indolent sentries lounging under the Giottesquely frescoed arch of Porta San Giorgio, into the open road. By this time I fancy the landscape will have got the better of history in the interest of any amateur, and he will give but a casual glance at Michael Angelo's bastions or towers, and will abandon himself altogether to the rapture of that scene.

For my part, I cannot tell whether I am more blest in the varieties of effect which every step of the descent outside the wall reveals in the city and its river and valley, or in the near olive orchards, gray in the sun, and the cypresses, intensely black against the sky. The road next the wall is bordered by a tangle of blackberry vines, which the amiable Florentine winter has not had the harshness to rob of their leaves; they hang green from the canes, on which one might almost hope to find some berries. The lizards, basking in the warm dust, rustle away among them at my approach, and up the path comes a gentleman in the company of two small terrier dogs, whose little bells finely tinkle us they advance. It would be hard to say just how these gave the final touch to my satisfaction with a prospect in which everything glistened and sparkled as far as the snows of Vallombrosa, lustrous along the horizon; but the reader ought to understand.

## XXII.

I was instructed by the friend in whose tutelage I was pursuing with so much passion my search for historical localities that I had better not give myself quite away to either the associations or the landscapes at Porta San Giorgio, but wait till I visited San Miniatio. Afterward I was glad that I did so, for that is certainly the point from which best to enjoy both. The day of our visit was gray and overcast, but the air was clear, and nothing was lost to the eye among the objects distinct in line and color, almost as far as it could reach. We went out of the famous Porta Romana, by which so much history enters and issues that if the customs officers there were not the most circumspect of men, they never could get round among the peasants' carts to tax their wine and oil without trampling a multitude of august and pathetic presences under foot. One shudders at the rate at which one's *cocchiere* dashes through the Past thronging the lofty archway, and scatters its phantoms right and left with loud explosions of his whip. Outside it is somewhat better, among the curves and slopes of the beautiful suburban avenues, with which Florence was adorned to be the capital of Italy twenty years ago. But here, too, history thickens upon you, even if you know it but a little; it springs from the soil that looks so red and poor, and seems to fill the air. In no other space, it seems to me, do the great events stand so dense as in that city and the circuit of its hills; so that, for mere pleasure in its beauty, the sense of its surpassing loveliness, perhaps one had better not know the history of Florence at all. As little as I knew it, I was terribly incommoded by it; and that morning, when I drove up to San Miniato to "realize" the siege of Florence, keeping a sharp eye out for Montici, where Sciarra Colonna had his quarters, and the range of hills whence the imperial forces joined in the chorus of his cannon battering the tower of the church,

I would far rather have been an unpremeditating listener
to the poem of Browning which the friend in the carriage
with me was repeating. The din of the guns drowned his
voice from time to time, and while he was trying to catch
a faded phrase, and going back and correcting himself, and
saying, "No – yes – no! That's it – no! Hold on – I have
it!" as people do in repeating poetry, my embattled fancy
was flying about over all the historic scene, sallying, repuls-
ing, defeating, succumbing; joining in the famous *camisada*
when the Florentines put their shirts on over their armor and
attacked the enemy's sleeping camp by night, and at the same
time playing ball down in the piazza of Santa Croce with
the Florentine youth in sheer contempt of the besiegers. It
was prodigiously fatiguing, and I fetched a long sigh of exhaustion as I dismounted at the steps of San Miniato, which
was the outpost of the Florentines, and walked tremulously
round it for a better view of the bower in whose top they
had planted their great gun. It was all battered there by the
enemy's shot aimed to dislodge the piece, and in the crum-
bling brickwork nodded tufts of grass and dry weeds in the
wind, like so many conceits of a frivolous tourist springing
from the tragic history it recorded. The apse of the church
below this tower is of the most satisfying golden brown in
color, and within, the church is what all the guide-books
know, but what I own I have forgotten. It is a very famous
temple, and every one goes to see it, for its frescos and mosaics and its peculiar beauty of architecture; and I dedicated
a moment of reverent silence to the memory of the poet
Giusti, whose monument was there. After four hundred
years of slavery, his pen was one of the keenest and bravest
of those which resumed the old Italian fight for freedom,

and he might have had a more adequate monument. I believe there is an insufficient statue, or perhaps it is only a bust, or may be a tablet with his face in bas-relief; but the modern Italians are not happy in their commemorations of the dead. The little Campo Santo at San Miniato is a place to make one laugh and cry with the hideous vulgarity of its realistic busts and its photographs set in the tombstones; and yet it is one of the least offensive in Italy. When I could escape from the fascination of its ugliness, I went and leaned with my friend on the parapet that encloses the Piazza Michelangelo, and took my fill of delight in the landscape. The city seemed to cover the whole plain beneath us with the swarm of its edifices, and the steely stretch of the Arno thrust through its whole length and spanned by its half-dozen bridges. The Duomo and the Palazzo Vecchio swelled up from the mass with a vastness which the distance seemed only to accent and reveal. To the northward showed the snowy tops of the Apennines, while on the nearer slopes of the soft brown hills flanking the wonderful valley the towns and villas hung densely drifted everywhere, and whitened the plain to its remotest purple.

I spare the reader the successive events which my unhappy acquaintance with the past obliged me to wait and see sweep over this mighty theatre. The winter was still in the wind that whistled round our lofty perch, and that must make the Piazza Michelangelo so delicious in the summer twilight; the bronze copy of the David in the centre of the square looked half frozen. The terrace is part of the system of embellishment and improvement of Florence for her brief supremacy as capital; and it is fitly called after Michael Angelo because it covers the site of so much work of his for her defence in the great siege. We looked about till we could endure the cold no longer, and then returned to our carriage. By this time the siege was over, and after a resistance of fifteen months we were betrayed by our leader Malatesta Baglioni, who could not resist the Pope's bribe. With the disgraceful facility of pleasure-seeking foreigners we instantly changed sides, and returned through the Porta Romana, which his treason opened, and, because it was so convenient, entered the city with a horde of other Spanish and German bigots and mercenaries that the empire had hurled against the stronghold of Italian liberty.

## XXIII.

Yet, once within the beloved walls, — I must still call them walls, though they are now razed to the ground and laid out in fine avenues, with a perpetual succession of horse-cars tinkling down their midst, — I was all Florentine again, and furious against the Medici, whom after a whole generation the holy league of the Emperor and the Pope had brought back in the person of the bastard Alessandro. They brought him back, of course, in prompt and explicit violation of their sacred word; and it seemed to me that I could not wait for his cousin Lorenzino to kill him, — such is the ferocity of the mildest tourist in the presence of occasions sufficiently remote. But surely if ever a man merited murder it was that brutal despot, whose tyrannies and excesses had something almost deliriously insolent in them, and who, crime for crime, seems to have preferred that which was most revolting. But I had to postpone this exemplary assassination till I could find the moment for visiting the Riccardi Palace,

in the name of which the fact of the elder Medicean residence is clouded. It has long been a public building, and now
some branch of the municipal government has its meetings
and offices there; but what the stranger commonly goes to
see is the chapel or oratory frescoed by Benozzo Gozzoli,
which is perhaps the most simply and satisfyingly lovely
little space that ever four walls enclosed. The sacred histories cover every inch of it with form and color; and if
it all remains in my memory a sensation of delight, rather
than anything more definite, that is perhaps a witness to the
efficacy with which the painter wrought. Serried ranks of
seraphs, peacock-plumed, and kneeling in prayer; garlands
of roses everywhere; contemporary Florentines on horse-
back, riding in the train of the Three Magi Kings under the
low boughs of trees; and birds fluttering through the dim,
mellow atmosphere, the whole set dense and close in an
opulent yet delicate fancifulness of design, – that is what
I recall, with a conviction of the idleness and absurdity of
recalling anything. It was like going out of doors to leave the
dusky splendor of this chapel, which was intended at first to
be seen only by the light of silver lamps, and come into the
great hall frescoed by Luca Giordano, where his classicis-
tic fables swim overhead in immeasurable light. They still
have the air, those boldly foreshortened and dramatically
postured figures, of being newly dashed on, – the work
of yesterday begun the day before; and they fill one with
an ineffable gayety: War, Pestilence, and Famine, no less
than Peace, Plenty, and Hygienic Plumbing, – if that was
one of the antithetical personages. Upon the whole, I think
the seventeenth century was more comfortable than the fifteenth, and that when men had fairly got their passions and

miseries impersonalized into allegory, they were in a state
to enjoy themselves much better than before. One can very
well imagine the old Cosimo who built this palace having
himself carried through its desolate magnificence, and crying that, now his son was dead, it was too big for his family;
but grief must have been a much politer and seemlier thing
in Florence when Luca Giordano painted the ceiling of the
great hall.

In the Duke Alessandro's time they had only got half-
way, and their hearts ached and burned in primitive fashion.
The revival of learning had brought them the consolation of
much classic example, both virtuous and vicious, but they
had not yet fully philosophized slavery into elegant passivity.
Even a reprobate like Lorenzino de' Medici – "the morrow
of a debauch," as De Musset calls him – had his head full of
the high Bonian fashion of finishing tyrants, and behaved as
much like a Greek as he could.

The Palazzo Riccardi now includes in its mass the site of
the house in which Lorenzino lived, as well as the narrow
street which formerly ran between his house and the palace
of the Medici; so that if you have ever so great a desire
to visit the very spot where Alessandro died that only too
insufficient death, you must wreak your frenzy upon a small
passage opening out of the present court. You enter this
from the modern liveliness of the Via Cavour, – in every
Italian city since the unification there is a Via Cavour, a
Via Garibaldi, and a Corso Vittorio Emmanuele, – and you
ordinarily linger for a moment among the Etruscan and
Roman marbles before paying your half franc and going
upstairs. There is a little confusion in this, but I think upon
the whole it heightens the effect; and the question whether

the custodian can change a piece of twenty francs, debating itself all the time in the mind of the amateur of tyrannicide, sharpens his impatience, while he turns aside into the street which no longer exists, and mounts the phantom stairs to the vanished chamber of the demolished house, where the Duke is waiting for the Lady Ginori, as he believes, but really for his death. No one, I think, claims that he was a demon less infernal than Lorenzino makes him out in that strange Apology of his, in which he justifies himself to posterity by appeals to antiquity. "Alessandro," he says, "went far beyond Phalaris in cruelty, because, whereas Phalaris justly punished Perillus for his cruel invention for miserably tormenting and destroying men in his brazen Bull, Alessandro would have rewarded him if he had lived in his time, for he was himself always thinking out new sorts of tortures and deaths, like building men up alive in places so narrow that they could not turn or move, but might be said to be built in as a part of the wall of brick and stone, and in that state feeding them and prolonging their misery as much as possible, the monster not satisfying himself with the mere death of his people; so that the seven years of his reign, for debauchery, for avarice and cruelty, may be compared with seven others of Nero, of Caligula, or of Phalaris, choosing the most abominable of their whole lives, in proportion, of course, of the city to the empire; for in that time so many citizens will be found to have been driven from their country, and persecuted, and murdered in exile, and so many beheaded without trial and without cause, and only for empty suspicion, and for words of no importance, and others poisoned or slain by his own hand, or his satellites, merely that they might not put him to shame before certain persons, for the condition in which he

was born and reared; and so many extortions and robberies
will be found to have been committed, so many adulteries,
so many violences, not only in things profane but in sacred
also, that it will be difficult to decide whether the tyrant was
more atrocious and impious, or the Florentine people more
patient and vile. . . . And if Timoleon was forced to kill his
own brother to liberate his country, and was so much praised
and celebrated for it, and still is so, what authority have the
malevolent to blame me? But in regard to killing one who
trusted me (which I do not allow I have done), I say that if I
had done it in this case, and if I could not have accomplished
it otherwise, I should have done it. . . . That he was not of
the house of Medici and my kinsman is manifest, for he was
born of a woman of base condition, from Castelvecchi in the
Romagna, who lived in the house of the Duke Lorenzo [of
Urbino], and was employed in the most menial services, and
married to a coachman. . . . He [Alessandro] left her to work
in the fields, so that those citizens of ours who had fled from
the tyrant's avarice and cruelty in the city determined to
conduct her to the Emperor at Naples, to show his Majesty
whence came the man he thought fit to rule Florence. Then
Alessandro, forgetting his duty in his shame, and the love
for his mother, which indeed he never had, and through an
inborn cruelty and ferocity, caused his mother to be killed
before she came to the Emperor's presence."

On the way up to the chamber to which the dwarfish,
sickly little tyrannicide has lured his prey, the most dramatic
moment occurs. He stops the bold ruffian whom he has got
to do him the pleasure of a certain unspecified homicide,
in requital of the good turn by which he once saved his
life, and whispers to him, "It is the Duke!" Scoronconcolo,

who had merely counted on an every-day murder, falters in dismay. But he recovers himself: "Here we are; go ahead, if it were the devil himself!" And after that he has no more compunction in the affair than if it were the butchery of a simple citizen. The Duke is lying there on the bed in the dark, and Lorenzino bends over him with "Are you asleep, sir?" and drives his sword, shortened to half length, through him, but the Duke springs up, and crying out, "I did not expect this of thee!" makes a fight for his life that tasks the full strength of the assassins, and covers the chamber with blood. When the work is done, Lorenzino draws the curtains round the bed again, and pins a Latin verse to them explaining that he did it for love of country and the thirst for glory.

## XXIV.

Is it perhaps all a good deal too much like a stage-play? Or is it that stage-plays are too much like facts of this sort? If it were at the theatre, one could go away, deploring the bloodshed, of course, but comforted by the justice done on an execrable wretch, the murderer of his own mother, and the pollution of every life that he touched. But if it is history we have been reading, we must turn the next page and see the city filled with troops by the Medici and their friends, and another of the race established in power before the people know that the Duke is dead. Clearly, poetical justice is not the justice of God. If it were, the Florentines would have had the republic again at once. Lorenzino, instead of being assassinated in Venice, on his way to see a lady, by the

emissaries of the Medici, would have satisfied public decorum by going through the form of a trial, and would then
have accepted some official employment and made a good
end. Yet the seven Medicean dukes who followed Alessandro were so variously bad for the most part that it seems
impious to regard them as part of the design of Providence.
How, then, did they come to be? Is it possible that sometimes evil prevails by its superior force in the universe? We
must suppose that it took seven Medicean despots and as
many more of the house of Lorraine and Austria to iron the
Florentines out to the flat and polished peacefulness of their
modern effect. Of course, the commonwealth could not go
on in the old way; but was it worse at its worst than the
tyranny that destroyed it? I am afraid we must allow that
it was more impossible. People are not put into the world
merely to love their country; they must have peace. True
freedom is only a means to peace; and if such freedom as
they have will not give them peace, then they must accept it
from slavery. It is always to be remembered that the great
body of men are not affected by oppressions that involve
the happiness of the magnanimous few; the affair of most
men is mainly to be sheltered and victualled and allowed to
prosper and bring up their families. Yet when one thinks of
the sacrifices made to perpetuate popular rule in Florence,
one's heart is wrung in indignant sympathy with the hearts
that broke for it. Of course, one must, in order to experience this emotion, put out of his mind certain facts, as that
there never was freedom for more than one party at a time
under the old commonwealth; that as soon as one party
came into power the other was driven out of the city; and
that even within the triumphant party every soul seemed

corroded by envy and distrust of every other. There is, to
be sure, the consoling reflection that the popular party was
always the most generous and liberal, and that the oppression of all parties under the despotism was not exactly an
improvement on the oppression of one. With this thought
kept before you vividly, and with those facts blinked, you
may go, for example, into the Medici Chapel of San Lorenzo
and make pretty sure of your pang in the presence of those
solemn figures of Michael Angelo's, where his Night seems
to have his words of grief for the loss of liberty upon her
lips:

> "'T is sweet to sleep, sweeter of stone to be,
>     And while endure the infamy and woe,
> For me 't is happiness not to feel or see.
>     Do not awake me therefore. Ah, speak low!"

## XXV.

Those words of Michael Angelo's answer to Strozzi's civil
verses on his Day and Night are nobly simple, and of a
colloquial and natural pitch to which their author seldom
condescended in sculpture. Even the Day is too muscularly
awaking and the Night too anatomically sleeping for the
spectator's perfect loss of himself in the sculptor's thought;
but the figures are so famous that it is hard to reconcile one's
self to the fact that they do not celebrate the memory of the
greatest Medici. That Giuliano whom we see in the chapel
there is little known to history; of that Lorenzo, history
chiefly remembers that he was the father of Alessandro,
whom we have seen slain, and of Catharine de' Medici.

Some people may think this enough; but we ought to read the lives of the other Medici before deciding. Another thing to guard against in that chapel is the cold; and, in fact, one ought to go well wrapped up in visiting any of the in-door monuments of Florence. Santa Croce, for example, is a temple whose rigors I should not like to encounter again in January, especially if the day be fine without. Then the sun streams in with a deceitful warmth through the mellow blazon of the windows, and the crone, with her scaldino at the door, has the air almost of sitting by a register. But it is all an illusion. By the time you have gone the round of the strutting and mincing allegories, and the pompous effigies with which art here, as everywhere, renders death ridiculous, you have scarcely the courage to penetrate to those remote chapels where the Giotto frescos are. Or if you do, you shiver round among them with no more pleasure in them than if they were so many boreal lights. Vague they are, indeed, and spectral enough, those faded histories of John the Baptist, and John the Evangelist, and St. Francis of Assisi, and as far from us, morally, as anything at the pole; so that the honest sufferer, who feels himself taking cold in his bare head, would blush for his absurdity in pretending to get any comfort or joy from them, if all the available blood in his body were not then concentrated in the tip of his nose. For my part, I marvelled at myself for being led, even temporarily, into temptation of that sort; and it soon came to my putting my book under my arm and my hands in my pockets, and, with a priest's silken skull-cap on my head, sauntering among those works of art with no more sense of obligation to them than if I were their contemporary. It is well, if possible, to have some one with you to look at the book, and see what the works are and the authors. But nothing of it is comparable to getting out into the open piazza again, where the sun is so warm, – though not so warm as it looks.

It suffices for the Italians, however, who are greedy in nothing and do not require to be warmed through, any more than to be fed full. The wonder of their temperance comes back with perpetual surprise to the gluttonous Northern nature. Their shyness of your fire, their gentle deprecation of your out-of-hours hospitality, amuse as freshly as at first; and the reader who has not known the fact must imagine the well-dressed throng in the Florentine street more meagrely breakfasted and lunched than anything but destitution with us, and protected against the cold in-doors by nothing but the clothes which are much more efficient without.

**XXVI.**

What strikes one first in the Florentine crowd is that it *is* so well dressed. I do not mean that the average of fashion is so great as with us, but that the average of raggedness is less. Venice, when I saw it again, seemed in tatters, but, so far as I can remember, Florence was not even patched; and this, in spite of the talk one constantly hears of the poverty which has befallen the city since the removal of the capital to Borne. All classes are said to feel this adversity more or less, but none of them show it on the street; beggary itself is silenced to the invisible speech which one sees moving the lips of the old women who steal an open palm towards you at the church doors. Florence is not only better dressed on the average than Boston, but, with little over half the population, there are, I should think, nearly twice as many private carriages in the former city. I am not going beyond the most non-committal *si dice* in any study of the Florentine civilization, and I know no more than that it is said (as it has been said ever since the first northern tourist discovered them) that they will starve themselves at home to make a show abroad. But if they do not invite the observer to share their domestic self-denial, – and it is said that they do not, even when he has long ceased to be a passing stranger, – I do not see why he should complain. For my part their abstemiousness cost me no sacrifice, and I found a great deal of pleasure in looking at the turnouts in the Cascine, and at the fur-lined coats in the streets and piazzas. They are always great wearers of fur in the south, but I think it is less fashionable than it used to be in Italy. The younger swells did not wear it in Florence, but now and then I met an elderly gentleman, slim, tall, with an iron-gray mustache, who, in folding his long fur-lined overcoat loosely about him as he walked, had a gratifying effect of being an ancestral portrait of himself; and with all persons and classes content to come short of recent fashion, fur is the most popular wear for winter. Each has it in such measure as he may; and one day in the Piazza della Signoria, when there was for some reason an assemblage of market-folk there, every man had hanging operatically from his shoulder an overcoat with cheap fur collar and cuffs. They were all babbling and gesticulating with an impassioned amiability, and their voices filled the place with a leafy rustling which it must have known so often in the old times, when the Florentines came together there to govern Florence. One ought not, I suppose, to imagine them always too grimly bent on public business in those times. They must have got a great deal of fun out of it,

in the long run, as well as trouble, and must have enjoyed
sharpening their wits upon one another vastly.

The presence now of all those busy-tongued people —
bargaining or gossiping, whichever they were — gave its
own touch to the peculiarly noble effect of the piazza, as it
rose before me from the gentle slope of the Via Borgo dei
Greci. I was coming back from that visit to Santa Croce, of
which I have tried to give the sentiment, and I was resentfully
tingling still with the cold, and the displeasure of a backward
glance at the brand-new ugliness of the façade, and of the
big clumsy Dante on his pedestal before it, when all my
burden suddenly lifted from me, as if nothing could resist
the spring of that buoyant air. It was too much for even the
dull, vague rage I felt at having voluntarily gone through that
dreary old farce of old-master doing again, in which the man
only averagely instructed in the history of art is at his last
extreme of insincerity, weariness, and degradation, — the
ridiculous and miserable slave of the guide-book asterisks
marking this or that thing as worth seeing. All seemed to
rise and float away with the thin clouds, chasing one another
across the generous space of afternoon sky which the piazza
opened to the vision; and my spirit rose as light as the lion
of the Republic, which capers so nimbly up the staff on top
of the palace tower.

There is something fine in the old piazza being still true to
the popular and even plebeian use. In narrow and crowded
Florence, one might have supposed that fashion would have
tried to possess itself of the place, after the public palace
became the residence of the Medici; but it seems not to have
changed its ancient character. It is now the starting-point
of a line of omnibuses; a rank of cabs surrounds the base

of Cosimo's equestrian statue; the lottery is drawn on the platform in front of the palace; second-rate shops of all sorts face it from two sides, and the restaurants and cafés of the neighborhood are inferior. But this unambitious environment leaves the observer all the freer to his impressions of the local art, the groups of the Loggia dei Lanzi, the symmetrical stretch of the Portico degli Uffizzi, and, best of all, the great, bold, irregular mass of the old palace itself, beautiful as some rugged natural object is beautiful, and with the kindliness of nature in it. Plenty of men have been hung from its windows, plenty dashed from its turrets, slain at its base, torn in pieces, cruelly martyred before it; the wild passions of the human heart have beaten against it like billows; it has faced every violent crime and outbreak. And yet it is sacred, and the scene is sacred, to all who hope for their kind; for there, in some sort, century after century, the purpose of popular sovereignty – the rule of all by the most – struggled to fulfil itself, purblindly, bloodily, ruthlessly, but never ignobly, and inspired by an instinct only less strong than the love of life. There is nothing superfine, nothing of the *salon* about the place, nothing of the beauty of Piazza San Marco at Venice, which expresses the elegance of an oligarchy and suggests the dapper perfection of an aristocracy in decay; it is loud with wheels and hoofs, and busy with commerce, and it has a certain ineffaceable rudeness and unfinish like the structure of a democratic state.

## XXVII.

When Cosimo I, who succeeded Alessandro, moved his residence from the family seat of the Medici to the Palazzo

Vecchio, it was as if he were planting his foot on the very neck of Florentine liberty. He ground his iron heel in deeply; the prostrate city hardly stirred afterwards. One sees what a potent and valiant man he was from the terrible face of the bronze bust by Benvenuto Cellini, now in the Bargello Museum; but the world, going about its business these many generations, remembers him chiefly by a horrid crime – the murder of his son in the presence of the boy's mother. Yet he was not only a great warrior and wild beast; he befriended letters, endowed universities, founded academies, encouraged printing; he adorned his capital with statues and public edifices; he enlarged and enriched the Palazzo Vecchio; he bought Luca Pitti's palace, and built the Uffizzi, thus securing the eternal gratitude of the tourists who visit these galleries, and have something to talk about at the *table d'hôte*. It was he who patronized Benvenuto Cellini, and got him to make his Perseus in the Loggia de' Lanzi; he built the fishermen's arcade in the Mercato Vecchio, and the fine loggia of the Mercato Nuovo; he established the General Archives, and reformed the laws and the public employments; he created Leghorn, and throughout Tuscany, which his arms had united under his rule, he promoted the material welfare of his people, after the manner of tyrants when they do not happen to be also fools.

His care of them in other respects may be judged from the fact that he established two official spies in each of the fifty wards of the city, whose business it was to keep him informed of the smallest events, and all that went on in the houses and streets, together with their conjectures and suspicions. He did not neglect his people in any way; and

he not only built all those fine public edifices in Florence,—
having merely to put his hand in his people's pocket and
do it, and then take the credit of them, – but he seems
to have loved to adorn it with that terrible face of his on
many busts and statues. Its ferocity, as Benvenuto Cellini
has frankly recorded it, and as it betrays itself in all the
effigies, is something to appall us still; and whether the
story is true or not, you see in it a man capable of striking
his son dead in his mother's arms. To be sure, Garzia was
not Cosimo's favorite, and, like a Medici, he had killed his
brother; but he was a boy, and when his father came to Pisa
to find him, where he had taken refuge with his mother, he
threw himself at Cosimo's feet and implored forgiveness.
"I want no Cains in my family!" said the father, and struck
him with the dagger which he had kept hidden in his breast.
"Mother! Mother!" gasped the boy, and fell dead in the arms
of the hapless woman, who had urged him to trust in his
father's mercy. She threw herself on the bed where they
laid her dead son, and never looked on the light again. Some
say she died of grief, some that she starved herself; in a
week she died, and was carried with her two children to
Florence, where it was presently made known that all three
had fallen victims to the bad air of the Maremma. She was
the daughter of a Spanish king, and eight years after her
death her husband married the vulgar and ignoble woman
who had long been his mistress. This woman was young,
handsome, full of life, and she queened it absolutely over
the last days of the bloody tyrant. His excesses had broken
Cosimo with premature decrepitude; he was helpless in the
hands of this creature, from whom his son tried to separate
him in vain; and he was two years in dying, after the palsy

had deprived him of speech and motion, but left him able
to think and to remember!

The son was that Francesco I. who is chiefly known to
fame as the lover and then the husband of Bianca Cappello, —
to so little may a sovereign prince come in the crowded and
busy mind of after-time. This grand duke had his courts
and his camps, his tribunals and audiences, his shows of
authority and government; but what we see of him at this
distance is the luxurious and lawless youth, sated with every indulgence, riding listlessly by under the window of
the Venetian girl who eloped with the Florentine banker's
clerk from her father's palace in the lagoons, and is now
the household drudge of her husband's family in Florence.
She is looking out of the window that looks on Savonarola's
convent, in the tallest of the stupid, commonplace houses
that confront it across the square; and we see the prince and
her as their eyes meet, and the work is done in the gunpow-
dery way of southern passion. We see her again at the house
of those Spaniards in the Via de' Banchi, which leads out of
our Piazza Santa Maria Novella, from whence the Palazzo
Man-dragone is actually in sight; and the marchioness is
showing Bianca her jewels and — Wait a moment! There
is something else the marchioness wishes to show her; she
will go get it; and when the door reopens Francesco enters,
protesting his love, to Bianca's confusion, and no doubt to
her surprise; for how could she suppose he would be there?
We see her then at the head of the grand-ducal court, the
poor, plain Austrian wife thrust aside to die in neglect; and
then when Bianca's husband, whom his honors and good
fortune have rendered intolerably insolent, is slain by some
of the duke's gentlemen, — in the narrow street at Santo

Spirito, hard by the handsome house in Via Maggio which the duke has given her, — we see them married, and receiving in state the congratulations of Bianca's father and brother, who have come on a special embassy from Venice to proclaim the distinguished lady Daughter of the Republic, — and, of course, to withdraw the price hitherto set upon her head. We see them then in the sort of life which must always follow from such love, — the grand duke had spent three hundred thousand ducats in the celebration of his nuptials, — overeating, overdrinking, and seeking their gross pleasures amid the ruin of the State. We see them trying to palm off a supposititious child upon the Cardinal Ferdinand, who was the true heir to his brother, and would have none of his spurious nephew; and we see these three sitting down in the villa at Poggio a Caiano to the famous tart which Bianca, remembering the skill of her first married days, has made with her own hands, and which she courteously presses the Cardinal to be the first to partake of. He politely refuses, being provided with a ring of admirable convenience at that time in Italy, set with a stone that turned pale in the presence of poison. "Some one has to begin," cries Francesco, impatiently; and in spite of his wife's signs — she was probably treading on his foot under the table, and frowning at him — he ate of the mortal viand; and then in despair Bianca ate too, and they both died. Is this tart perhaps too much for the reader's digestion? There is another story, then, to the effect that the grand duke died of the same malarial fever that carried off his brothers Garzia and Giovanni, and Bianca perished of terror and apprehension; and there is still another story that the Cardinal poisoned them both. Let the reader take his choice of them; in any case, it is an end of

Francesco, whom, as I said, the world remembers so little else of.

It almost forgets that he was privy to the murder of his sister Isabella by her husband Paolo Orsini, and of his sister-in-law Eleonora by her husband Pietro de' Medici. The grand duke, who was then in the midst of his intrigue with Bianca, was naturally jealous of the purity of his family; and as it has never been denied that both of those unhappy ladies had wronged their husbands, I suppose he can be justified by the moralists who contend that what is a venial lapse in a man is worthy death, or something like it, in a woman. About the taking-off of Eleonora, however, there was something gross, Medicean, butcherly, which all must deprecate. She knew she was to be killed, poor woman, as soon as her intrigue was discovered to the grand duke; and one is not exactly able to sympathize with either the curiosity or the trepidation of that "celebrated Roman singer" who first tampered with the letter from her lover, intrusted to him, and then, terrified at its nature, gave it to Francesco. When her husband sent for her to come to him at his villa, she took leave of her child as for the last time, and Pietro met her in the dark of their chamber and plunged his dagger into her breast.

The affair of Isabella Orsini was managed with much greater taste, with a sort of homicidal grace, a sentiment, if one may so speak, worthy a Boman prince and a lady so accomplished. She was Cosimo's favorite, and she was beautiful, gifted, and learned, knowing music, knowing languages, and all the gentler arts; but one of her lovers had just killed her page, whom he was jealous of, and the scandal was very great, so that her brother, the grand duke, felt that he ought, for decency's sake, to send to Rome for her husband, and arrange her death with him. She, too, like Eleonora, had her forebodings, when Paolo Orsini asked her to their villa (it seems to have been the custom to devote the peaceful seclusion of the country to these domestic rites); but he did what he could to allay her fears by his affectionate gayety at supper, and his gift of either of those staghounds which he had brought in for her to choose from against the hunt planned for the morrow, as well as by the tender politeness with which he invited her to follow him to their room. At the door we may still see her pause, after so many years, and turn wistfully to her lady in waiting:

"Madonna Lucrezia, shall I go or shall I not go to my husband? What do you say?"

And Madonna Lucrezia Frescobaldi answers, with the irresponsible shrug which we can imagine: "Do what you like. Still, he is your husband!"

She enters, and Paolo Orsini, a prince and a gentleman, knows how to be as sweet as before, and without once passing from caresses to violence, has that silken cord about her neck.

Terrible stories, which I must try to excuse myself for telling the thousandth time. At least, I did not invent them. They are all part of the intimate life of the same family, and the reader must group them in his mind to get an idea of what Florence must have been under the first and second grand dukes. Cosimo is believed to have killed his son Garzia, who had stabbed his brother Giovanni. His son Pietro kills his wife, and his daughter Isabella is strangled by her husband, both murders being done with the knowledge and approval of the reigning prince. Francesco and Bianca his wife die of

poison intended for Ferdinand, or of poison given them by
him. On these facts throw the light of St. Bartholomew's
day in Paris, whither Catharine de' Medici, the cousin of
these homicides, had carried the methods and morals of her
family, and you begin to realize the Medici.

By what series of influences and accidents did any race
accumulate the enormous sum of evil which is but partly
represented in these crimes? By what process was that evil
worked out of the blood? Had it wreaked its terrible force
in violence, and did it then no longer exist, like some ex-
plosive which has been fired? These would be interesting
questions for the casuist; and doubtless such questions will
yet come to be studied with the same scientific minuteness
which is brought to the solution of contemporary social
problems. The Medici, a family of princes and criminals,
may come to be studied like the Jukes, a family of paupers
and criminals. What we know at present is, that the evil
in them did seem to die out in process of time; though, to
be sure, the Medici died with it. That Ferdinand who succeeded Francesco, whichever poisoned the other, did prove
a wise and beneficent ruler, filling Tuscany with good works,
moral and material, and, by his marriage with Catharine of
Lorraine, bringing that good race to Florence, where it afterwards reigned so long in the affections of the people. His
son Cosimo II was like him, but feebler, as a copy always
is, with a dominant desire to get the sepulchre of our Lord
away from the Turks to Florence, and long waging futile
war to that end. In the time of Ferdinand II, Tuscany, with
the rest of Italy, was wasted by the wars of the French,
Spaniards, and Germans, who found it convenient to fight
them out there, and by famine and pestilence. But the grand

duke was a well-meaning man enough; he protected the arts and sciences as he got the opportunity, and he did his best to protect Galileo against the Pope and the inquisitors Cosimo III, who followed him, was obliged to harass his subjects with taxes to repair the ruin of the wars in his father's reign; he was much given to works of piety, and he had a wife who hated him, and finally forsook him and went back to France, her own country. He reigned fifty years, and after him came his son Gian Gastone, the last of his line. He was a person, by all accounts, who wished men well enough, but, knowing himself destined to leave no heir to the throne, was disposed rather to enjoy what was left of his life than trouble himself about the affairs of state. Germany, France, England, and Holland had already provided him with a successor, by the treaty of London, in 1718; and when Gian Gastone died, in 1737, Francis II of Lorraine became Grand Duke of Tuscany.

## XXVIII.

Under the later Medici the Florentines were drawing towards the long quiet which they enjoyed under their Lorrainese dukes – the first of whom, as is well known, left being their duke to go and be husband of Maria Theresa and emperor consort. Their son, Pietro Leopoldo, succeeded him in Tuscany, and became the author of reforms in the civil, criminal, and ecclesiastical law, which then astonished all Europe, and which tardy civilization still lags behind in some things. For example, Leopold found that the abolition of the death penalty resulted not in more, but in fewer crimes of violence; yet the law continues to kill murderers, even in Massachusetts.

He lived to see the outbreak of the French revolution, and his son, Ferdinand III, was driven out by the forces of the Republic in 1796, after which Tuscany rapidly underwent the Napoleonic metamorphoses, and was republican under the Directory, regal under Lodovico I, Bonaparte's king of Etruria, and grand-ducal under Napoleon's sister, Elisa Bacciocchi. Then, in 1816, Ferdinand III came back, and he and his descendants reigned till 1848, when Leopold II was driven out, to return the next year with the Austrians. Ten years later he again retired, and in 1860 Tuscany united herself by popular vote to the kingdom of Italy, of which Florence became the capital, and so remained till the French evacuated Rome in 1871.

The time from the restoration of Ferdinand III till the first expulsion of Leopold II must always be attractive to the student of Italian civilization as the period in which the milder Lorrainese traditions permitted the germs of Italian literature to live in Florence, while everywhere else the native and foreign despotisms sought diligently to destroy them, instinctively knowing them to be the germs of Italian liberty and nationality; but I confess that the time of the first Leopold's reign has a greater charm for my fancy. It is like a long stretch of sunshine in that lurid, war-clouded landscape of history, full of repose and genial, beneficent growth. For twenty-five years, apparently, the good prince got up at six o'clock in the morning, and dried the tears of his people. To be more specific, he "formed the generous project," according to Signor Bacciotti, by whose "Firenze Illustrata" I would not thanklessly profit, "of restoring

Tuscany to her original happy state" – which, I think, must have been prehistoric. "His first occupation was to reform the laws, simplifying the civil and mitigating the criminal; and the volumes are ten that contain his wise statutes, edicts, and decrees. In his time, ten years passed in which no drop of blood was shed on the scaffold. Prisoners suffered no corporeal penalty but the loss of liberty. The amelioration of the laws improved the public morals; grave crimes, after the abolition of the cruel punishments, became rare, and for three months at one period the prisons of Tuscany remained empty. The hospitals that Leopold founded, and the order and propriety in which he kept them, justly entitled him to the name of Father of the Poor. The education he gave his children aimed to render them compassionate and beneficent to their fellow-beings, and to make them men rather than princes. An illustrious Englishman, then living in Florence, and consequently an eye-witness, wrote of him: 'Leopold loves his people. He has abolished all the imposts which were not necessary; he has dismissed nearly all his soldiers; he has destroyed the fortifications of Pisa, whose maintenance was extremely expensive, overthrowing the stones that devoured men. He observed that his court concealed him from his people; he no longer has a court. He has established manufactures, and opened superb roads at his own cost, and founded hospitals. These might be called, in Tuscany, the palaces of the grand duke. I visited them, and found throughout cleanliness, order, and delicate and attentive treatment; I saw sick old men, who were cared for as if by their own sons; helpless children watched over with a mother's care; and that luxury of pity and humanity brought happy tears to my eyes. The prince often repairs to these abodes of sorrow and pain, and never quits them without leaving joy behind him, and coming away loaded with blessings: you might fancy you heard the expression of a happy people's gratitude, but that hymn rises from a hospital. The palace of Leopold, like the churches, is open to all without distinction; three days of the week are devoted to one class of persons; it is not that of the great, the rich, the artists, the foreigners; it is that of the unfortunate! In many countries, commerce and industry have become the patrimony of the few: in Tuscany, all that know how may do; there is but one exclusive privilege, – ability. Leopold has enriched the year with a great number of work-days, which he took from idleness and gave back to agriculture, to the arts, to good morals. . . . The grand duke always rises before the sun, and when that beneficent star rejoices nature with its rays, the good prince has already dried many tears. . . . Leopold is happy, because his people are happy; he believes in God; and what must be his satisfaction when, before closing his eyes at night, before permitting himself to sleep, he renders an account to the Supreme Being of the happiness of a million of subjects during the course of the day!'"

English which has once been Italian acquires an emotionality which it does not perhaps wholly lose in returning to itself; and I am not sure that the language of the illustrious stranger, whom I quote at second hand, has not kept some terms which are native to Signor Bacciotti rather than himself. But it must be remembered that he was an eighteenth-century Englishman, and perhaps expressed himself much in this way. The picture he draws, if a little too idyllic, too pastoral, too operatic, for our realization, must still have been founded on fact, and I hope it is at least as true as those which commemorate the atrocities of the Medic. At any rate it is delightful, and one may as probably derive the softness of the modern Florentine morals and manners from the benevolence of Leopold as from the ferocity of Cosimo. Considering what princes mostly were in the days when they could take themselves seriously, and still are now when I should think they would give themselves the wink on seeing their faces in the glass, I am willing to allow that kindly despot of a Leopold all the glory that any history may claim for him. He had the genius of humanity, and that is about the only kind of genius which is entitled to reverence in this world. If he perhaps conceived of men as his children rather than his brothers still he wished them well and did them all the good he knew how. After a hundred years it must be allowed that we have made a considerable advance beyond him – in theory.

## XXIX.

What society in Florence may now be like underneath its superficial effect of gentleness and placidity, the stranger, who reflects how little any one really knows of his native civilization, will carefully guard himself from saying upon his own authority. From the report of others, of people who had lived long in Florence and were qualified in that degree to speak, one might say a great deal, – a great deal that would be more and less than true. A brilliant and accomplished writer, a stranger naturalized by many years' sojourn, and of an imaginable intimacy with his subject, sometimes spoke to me of a decay of manners which he had noticed in his

time: the peasants no longer saluted persons of civil condition in meeting them; the young nobles, if asked to a ball,
ascertained that there was going to be supper before accept-
ing. I could not find these instances very shocking, upon
reflection; and I was not astonished to hear that the sort of
rich American girls who form the chase of young Florentine
noblemen show themselves indifferent to untitled persons.
There was something more of instruction in the fact that
these fortune-hunters care absolutely nothing for youth or
beauty, wit or character, in their prey, and ask nothing
but money. This implies certain other facts, – certain com-
pensations and consolations, which the American girl with
her heart set upon an historical name would be the last to
consider. What interested me more was the witness which
this gentleman bore, with others, to the excellent stuff of
the peasants, whom he declared good and honest, and full
of simple, kindly force and uprightness. The citizen class,
on the other hand, was unenlightened and narrow-minded,
and very selfish towards those beneath them; he believed
that a peasant, for example, who cast his lot in the city,
would encounter great unfriendliness in them if he showed
the desire and the ability to rise above his original station.
Both from this observer, and from other foreigners resident
in Florence, I heard that the Italian nobility are quite apart
from the national life; they have no political influence, and
are scarcely a social power; there are, indeed, but three of
the old noble families founded by the German emperors
remaining, – the Ricasoli, the Gherardeschi, and the Stufe;
and a title counts absolutely for nothing with the Italians. At
the same time a Corsini was syndic of Florence; all the dead
walls invited me to "vote for Peruzzi" in the approaching

election for deputy, and at the last election a Ginori had been chosen. It is very hard to know about these things, and I am not saying my informants were wrong; but it is right to oppose to theirs the declaration of the intelligent and sympathetic scholar with whom I took my walks about Florence, and who said that there was great good-will between the people and the historical families, who were in thorough accord with the national aspirations and endeavors. Again, I say, it is difficult to know the truth; but happily the truth in this case is not important.

One of the few acquaintances I made with Italians outside of the English-speaking circles was that of a tradesman who, in the intervals of business, was reading Shakespeare in English, and — if I may say it — "Venetian Life." I think some Americans had lent him the latter classic. I did not learn from him that many other Florentine tradesmen gave their leisure to the same literature; in fact, I inferred that, generally speaking, there was not much interest in any sort of literature among the Florentines; and I only mention him in the hope of throwing some light upon the problem with which we are playing. He took me one night to the Literary Club, of which he was a member, and of which the Marchese Ricci is president; and I could not see that any presentation could have availed me more than his with that nobleman or the other nobleman who was secretary. The president shook my hand in a friendly despair, perfectly evident, of getting upon any common ground with me; and the secretary, after asking me if I knew Doctor Holmes, had an amiable effect of being cast away upon the sea of American literature. These gentlemen, as I understood, came every week to the club, and assisted at its entertainments, which were sometimes concerts, sometimes lectures and recitations, and sometimes conversation merely, for which I found the empty chairs, on my entrance, arranged in groups of threes and fives about the floor, with an air perhaps of too great social premeditation. Presently there was playing on the piano, and at the end the president shook hands with the performer. If there was anything of the snobbishness which poisons such intercourse for our race, I could not see it. May be snobbishness, like gentlemanliness, is not appreciable from one race to another.

## XXX.

My acquaintance, whom I should grieve to make in any sort a victim by my personalities, did me the pleasure to take me over the little ancestral farm which he holds just beyond one of the gates; and thus I got at one of the homely aspects of life which the stranger is commonly kept aloof from. A narrow lane, in which some boys were pitching stones for quoits in the soft Sunday afternoon sunshine, led up from the street to the farm-house, where one wandering roof covered house, stables, and offices with its mellow expanse of brown tiles. A door opening flush upon the lane admitted us to the picturesque interior, which was divided into the quarters of the farmer and his family, and the apartment which the owner occupied during the summer heats. This contained half a dozen pleasant rooms, chief of which was the library, overflowing with books representing all the rich past of Italian literature in poetry, history, and philosophy, – the collections of my host's father and grandfather. On the table he opened a bottle of the wine made on his farm; and then he

took me up to the terrace at the house-top for the beautiful
view of the city, and the mountains beyond it, streaked with
snow. The floor of the terrace, which, like all the floors of the
house, was of brick, was heaped with olives from the orchard
on the hillside which bounded the little farm; but I could see
from this point how it was otherwise almost wholly devoted
to market-gardening. The grass keeps green all winter long
at Florence, not growing, but never withering; and there
were several sorts of vegetables in view, in the same sort of
dreamy arrest. Between the rows of cabbages I noticed the
trenches for irrigation; and I lost my heart to the wide, deep
well under the shed-roof below, with a wheel, picturesque
as a mill-wheel, for pumping water into these trenches. The
farm implements and heavier household utensils were kept
in order here; and among the latter was a large wash-tub of
fine earthenware, which had been in use there for a hundred
and fifty years. My friend led the way up the slopes of his
olive-orchard, where some olives still lingered among the
willow-like leaves, and rewarded my curious palate with
the insipidity of the olive which has not been salted. Then
we returned to the house, and explored the cow-stables,
where the well-kept Italian kine between their stone walls
were much warmer than most Italian Christians in Florence.
In a large room next the stable and behind the kitchen the
farm-people were assembled, men, women, and children,
in their Sunday best, who all stood up when we came in, –
all but two very old men, who sat in the chimney and held
out their hands over the fire that sent its smoke up between
them. Their eyes were bleared with age, and I doubt if they
made out what it was all about; but they croaked back a
pleasant answer to my host's salutation, and then let their

mouths fall open again and kept their hands stretched over the fire. It would be very hard to say just why these old men were such a pleasure to me.

XXXI.

One January afternoon I idled into the Baptistery, to take my chance of seeing some little one made a Christian, where so many babes, afterwards memorable for good and evil, had been baptized; and, to be sure, there was the conventional Italian infant of civil condition tied up tight in the swathing of its civilization, perfectly quiescent, except for its feebly wiggling arms, and undergoing the rite with national patience. It lay in the arms of a half-grown boy, probably its brother, and there were the father and the nurse; the mother of so young a child could not come, of course. The officiating priest, with spectacles dropped quite to the point of his nose, mumbled the rite from his book, and the assistant, with one hand in his pocket, held a negligently tilted taper in the other. Then the priest lifted the lid of the font in which many a renowned poet's, artist's, tyrant's, philanthropist's twisted little features were similarly reflected, and poured on the water, rapidly drying the poor little skull with a single wipe of a napkin; then the servant in attendance powdered the baby's head, and the group, grotesquely inattentive throughout to the sacred rite, dispersed, and left me and a German family who had looked on with murmurs of sympathy for the child to overmaster as we might any interest we had felt in a matter that had apparently not concerned them.

One is always coming upon this sort of thing in the Italian churches, this droll nonchalance in the midst of religious solemnities, which I suppose is promoted somewhat by the invasions of sightseeing everywhere. In the Church of the Badia at Florence, one day, the indifference of the tourists and the worshippers to one another's presence was carried to such a point that the boy who was showing the strangers about, and was consequently in their interest, drew the curtain of a picture, and then, with his back to a group of kneeling devotees, balanced himself on the chapel-rail and sat swinging his legs there, as if it had been a store-box on a curbstone.

Perhaps we do not sufficiently account for the domestication of the people of Latin countries in their every-day open church. They are quite at their ease there, whereas we are as unhappy in ours as if we were at an evening party; we wear all our good clothes, and they come into the houses of their Father in any rag they chance to have on, and are at home there. I have never seen a more careless and familiar group than that of which I was glad to form one, in the Church of Ognissanti, one day. I had gone, in my quality of American, to revere the tablet to Amerigo Vespucci which is there, and I found the great nave of the church occupied by workmen who were putting together the foundations of a catafalque, hammering away, and chatting cheerfully, with their mouths full of tacks and pins, and the funereal frippery of gold, black, and silver braid all about them. The church-beggars had left their posts to come and gossip with them, and the grandchildren of these old women were playing back and forth over the structure, unmolested by the workmen, and unawed either by the function going on in a distant chapel or by the theatrical magnificence of the sculptures around them and the fresco overhead, where a painted colonnade lifted another roof high above the real vault.

I liked all this, and I could not pass a church door without the wish to go in, not only for the pictures or statues one might see, but for the delightfully natural human beings one could always be sure of. Italy is above all lands the home of human nature, – simple, unabashed even in the presence of its Maker, who is probably not so much ashamed of his work as some would like to have us think. In the churches, the beggary which the civil government has disheartened almost out of existence in the streets is still fostered, and an aged crone with a scaldino in her lap, a tattered shawl over her head, and an outstretched, skinny palm, guards the portal of every sanctuary. She has her chair, and the church is literally her home; she does all but eat and sleep there. For the rest, these interiors had not so much novelty as the charm of old association for me. Either I had not enlarged my interests in the twenty years since I had known them, or else they had remained unchanged; there was the same old smell of incense, the same chill, the same warmth, the same mixture of glare and shadow. A function in progress at a remote altar, the tapers starring the distant dusk; the straggling tourists; the sacristan, eager, but not too persistent with his tale of some special attraction at one's elbow; the worshippers, all women or old men; a priest hurrying to or from the sacristy; the pictures, famous or unknown, above the side altars; the monuments, serious Gothic or strutting rococo, – all was there again, just as it used to be.

But the thing that was really novel to me, who found the churches of 1883 in Florence so like the churches of 1863 in Venice, was the loveliness of the deserted cloisters belonging to so many of the former. These enclose nearly always a grass-grown space, where daisies and dandelions began to abound with the earliest consent of spring. Most public places and edifices in Italy have been so much photographed that few have any surprise left in them: one is sure that one has seen them before; but the cloisters are not yet the prey of this sort of pre-acquaintance. Whether the vaults and walls of the colonnades are beautifully frescoed, like those of Sta. Maria Novella or Sta. Annunziata or San Marco, or the place has no attraction but its grass and sculptured stone, it is charming; and these cloisters linger in my mind as something not less Florentine in character than the Ponte Vecchio or the Palazzo Publico. I remember particularly an evening effect in the cloister of Santa Annunziata, when the belfry in the corner, lifted aloft on its tower, showed with its pendulous bells like a great, graceful flower against the dome of the church behind it. The quiet in the place was almost sensible; the pale light, suffused with rose, had a delicate clearness; there was a little agreeable thrill of cold in the air; there could not have been a more refined moment's pleasure offered to a sympathetic tourist loitering slowly homeward to his hotel and its *table d'hôte*; and why we cannot have old cloisters in America, where we are getting everything that money can buy, is a question that must remain to vex us. A suppressed convent at the corner of, say, Clarendon Street and Commonwealth Avenue, where the new Brattle Street church is, would be a great pleasure on one's way home in the afternoon; but still I should lack the final satisfaction of dropping into the chapel of the Brothers of the Misericordia, a little farther on towards Santa Maria Novella.

The sentimentalist may despair as he pleases, and have his fill of panic about the threatened destruction of the Ponte Vecchio, but I say that while these brothers, "black-stoled, black-hooded, like a dream," continue to light the way to dusty death with their flaring torches through the streets of Florence, the mediæval tradition remains unbroken; Italy is still Italy. They knew better how to treat Death in the Middle Ages than we do now, with our vain profanation of flowers to his service, our loathsome dapperness of "burial caskets," and dress-coat and white tie for the dead. Those simple old Florentines, with their street wars, their pestilences, their manifold destructive violences, felt instinctively that he, the inexorable, was not to be hidden or palliated, not to be softened or prettified, or anywise made the best of, but was to be confessed in all his terrible gloom; and in this they found, not comfort, not alleviation, which time alone can give, but the anæsthesis of a freezing horror. Those masked and trailing sable figures, sweeping through the wide and narrow ways by night to the wild, long rhythm of their chant, in the red light of their streaming torches, and bearing the heavily draped bier in their midst, supremely awe the spectator, whose heart falters within him in the presence of that which alone is certain to be. I cannot say they are so effective by daylight, when they are carrying some sick or wounded person to the hospital; they have not their torches then, and the sun seems to take a cynical satisfaction in showing their robes to be merely of black glazed cotton. An anteroom of their chapel was fitted with locked and numbered drawers, where the brothers kept their robes; half a dozen coffin-shaped biers and litters stood about, and the floor was strewn with laurel-leaves, — I suppose because it was the festa of St. Sebastian.

## XXXII.

I do not know that the festas are noticeably fewer than they used to be in Italy. There are still enough of them to account for the delay in doing almost anything that has been promised to be done. The carnival came on scatteringly and reluctantly. A large sum of money which had been raised for its celebration was properly diverted to the relief of the sufferers by the inundations in Lombardy and Venetia, and the Florentines patiently set about being merry each on his own personal account. Not many were visibly merry, except in the way of business. The gentlemen of the operatic choruses clad themselves in stage-armor, and went about under the hotel-windows, playing and singing, and levying contributions on the inmates; here and there a white clown or a red devil figured through the streets; two or three carriages feebly attempted a *corso*, and there was an exciting rumor that *confetti* had been thrown from one of them: I did not see the *confetti*. There was for a long time doubt whether there was to be any *reglione* or ball on the last night of the carnival; but finally there were two of them: one of low degree at the Teatro Umberto, and one of more pretension at the Pergola Theatre. The latter presented an agreeable image of the carnival ball which has taken place in so many romances: the boxes filled with brilliantly dressed spectators, drinking

champagne; the floor covered with maskers, gibbering in
falsetto, dancing, capering, coquetting till daylight. This,
more than any other aspect of the carnival, seemed to give
one the worth of his money in tradition and association.
Not but that towards the end the masks increased in the
streets, and the shops where they sold costumes were very
gay; but the thing is dying out, as at least one Italian, in
whose veins the new wine of Progress had wrought, rejoiced to tell me. I do not know whether I rejoiced so much
to hear it; but I will own that I did not regret it a great
deal. Italy is now so much the sojourn of barbarians that
any such gayety must be brutalized by them, till the Italians turn from it in disgust. Then it must be remembered
that the carnival was fostered by their tyrants to corrupt
and enervate them; and I cannot wonder that their love of
Italy is wounded by it. They are trying to be men, and the
carnival is childish. I fancy that is the way my friend felt
about it.

## XXXIII.

After the churches, the Italians are most at home in their
theatres, and I went as often as I could to see them there,
preferably where they were giving the Stenterello plays.
Stenterello is the Florentine mask or type who survives the
older Italian comedy which Goldoni destroyed; and during
carnival he appeared in a great variety of characters at three
different theatres. He is always painted with wide wide purplish circles round his eyes, with an effect of goggles, and
a hare-lip; and his hair, caught into a queue behind, curls
up into a pigtail or his neck. With this face and this wig

he assumes any character the farce requires, and becomes delicious in proportion to his grotesque unfitness for it. The best Stenterello was an old man, since dead, who was very famous in the part. He was of such a sympathetic and lovely humor that your heart wanned to him the moment he came upon the stage, and when he opened his mouth, it scarcely mattered what he said: those Tuscan gutturals and abounding vowels as he uttered them were enough; but certainly to see him in "Stenterello and his own Corpse," or "Stenterello Umbrella-mender," or "Stenterello Quack Doctor" was one of the great and simple pleasures. He was an actor who united the quaintness of Jefferson to the sweetness of Warren; in his wildest burlesque he was so true to nature in every touch and accent, that I wanted to sit there and spend my life in the innocent folly of enjoying him. Apparently, the rest of the audience desired the same. Nowhere, even in Italy, was the sense of rest from all the hurrying, great weary world outside so full as in certain moments of this Stenterello's absurdity at the Teatro Rossini, which was not otherwise a comfortable place. It was more like a section of a tunnel than like a theatre, being a rounded oblong, with the usual tiers of boxes, and the pit where there were seats in front, and two thirds of the space left free for standing behind. Every day there was a new bill, and I remember "Stenterello White Slave in America" and "Stenterello as Hamlet" among the attractions offered. In fact, he runs through an indefinite number of dramas, as Brighella, Arlecchino, Pantalone, Florindo, Rosaura, and the rest, appear and reappear in the comedies of Goldoni while he is temporizing with the old *commedia d'arte*, where he is at his best.

At what I may call the non-Stenterello theatres in
Florence, they were apt to give versions of the more
heart-breaking, vow-broken, French melodramas, though
occasionally there was a piece of Italian origin, generally
Giacosa's. But it seemed to me that there were now fewer
Italian plays given than there were twenty years ago; and
the opera season was almost as short and inclement as in
Boston.

## XXXIV.

I visited many places of amusements more popular than the
theatre, but I do not know that I can fitly offer them all
to the more polite and formal acquaintance of my readers,
whom I like always to figure as extremely well-behaved and
well-dressed persons. Which of these refined and fastidious
ladies and gentlemen shall I ask, for example, to go with
me to see a dying Zouave in wax in a booth at the Mercato
Vecchio, where there were other pathetic and monstrous
figures? At the door was a peasant-like personage who extolled himself from time to time as the inventor of a musical
instrument within, which he said he had exemplarily spent
his time in perfecting, instead of playing cards and *mora*. I
followed him inside with the crowd, chiefly soldiers, who
were in such overwhelming force that I was a little puzzled
to make out which corps and regiment I belonged to; but
I shared the common edification of the performance, when
our musical genius mounted a platform before a most in-
tricate instrument, which combined in itself, as he boasted,
the qualities of all other kinds of instruments. He shuffled
off his shoes and played its pedals with his bare feet, while

he sounded its pipes with his mouth, pounding a drum-attachment with one hand and scraping a violin-attachment with the other. I do not think the instrument will ever come into general use, and I have my doubts whether the inventor might not have better spared a moment or two of his time to *mora*. I enjoyed more a little vocal and acrobatic entertainment, where again I found myself in the midst of my brothers in arms. Civilians paid three cents to come in, but we military only two; and we had the best seats and smoked throughout the performance. This consisted of the feats of two nice, innocent-looking boys, who came out and tumbled, and of two sisters who sang a very long duet together, screeching the dialogue with which it was interspersed in the ear-piercingest voices; it represented a lovers' quarrel, and sounded very like some which I have heard on the roof and the back fences. But what I admired about this and other popular shows was the perfect propriety. At the circus in the Via Nazionale they had even a clown in a dress-coat.

Of course, the two iron tanks full of young crocodiles which I saw in a booth in our piazza classed themselves with great moral shows, because of their instructiveness. The water in which they lay soaking was warmed for them, and the chill was taken off the air by a sheet-iron stove, so that, upon the whole, these saurians had the most comfortable quarters in the whole shivering city. Although they had up a sign, "Animali pericolosi – non si toccano," nothing was apparently further from their thoughts than biting; they lay blinking in supreme content, and allowed a captain of horse to poke them with his finger throughout my stay, and were no more to be feared than that younger brother of theirs whom the showman went about with in his hand, lecturing on him; he was half-hatched from his native egg, and had been arrested and neatly varnished in the act for the astonishment of mankind.

<h2 style="text-align:center">XXXV.</h2>

We had the luck to be in Florence on the 25th of March, when one of the few surviving ecclesiastical shows peculiar to the city takes place. On that day a great multitude, chiefly of peasants from the surrounding country, assemble in front of the Duomo to see the explosion of the Car of the Pazzi. This car somehow celebrates the exploit of a crusading Pazzi, who broke off a piece of the Holy Sepulchre and brought it back to Florence with him; I could not learn just how or why, from the very scoffing and ironical little pamphlet which was sold in the crowd; but it is certain the car is covered with large fire-crackers, and if these explode successfully, the harvest for that year will be something remarkable. The car is stationed midway between the Duomo and the Baptistery, and the fire to set off the crackers is brought from the high altar by a pyrotechnic dove, which flies along a wire stretched for that purpose. If a mother with a sick child passes under the dove in its flight, the child is as good as cured.

The crowd was vast, packing the piazza outside around the car and the cathedral to its walls with all sorts and conditions of people, and every age and sex. An alley between the living walls was kept open under the wire, to let the archbishop, heading a procession of priests, go out to bless the car. When this was done, and he had returned within, we heard a faint pop at the high altar, and then a loud fizzing as the fiery dove came flying along the wire, showering sparks on every side; it rushed out to the car, and then fled back to the altar, amidst a most satisfactory banging of the firecrackers. It was not a very awful spectacle, and I suspect that my sarcastic pamphleteer's description was in the mood of most of the Florentines looking on, whatever the peasant thought. "'Now, Nina,' says the priest to the dove, 'we're almost ready, and look out how you come back, as well as go out That's a dear! It's for the good of all, and don't play me a trick – you understand? Ready! Are you ready? Well, then, – *Gloria in excelsis Deo*, – go, go, dear, and look out for your feathers! *Shhhhh!* pum, pum! Hurrah, little one! Now for the return! Here you come! *Shhhhh!* pum, pum, pum! And I don't care a fig for the rest!' And he goes on with his mass, while the crowd outside console themselves with the cracking and popping. Then those inside the church join those without, and follow the car up to the corner of the Pazzi palace, where the unexploded remnants are fired in honor of the family."

## XXXVI.

The civil rite now constitutes the only legal marriage in Italy, the blessing of the church going for nothing without it before the law; and I had had a curiosity to see the ceremony which one may see any day in the office of the syndic. The names of those intending matrimony are posted for a certain time on the base of the Public Palace, which gives everybody the opportunity of dedicating sonnets to them. The pay of a sonnet is one franc, so that the poorest couple can afford one; and I suppose the happy pair whom I saw waiting in the syndic's anteroom had provided themselves with one of these simple luxuries. They were sufficiently commonish, kindly faced young people, and they and their friends wore, with their best clothes, an air of natural excitement. A bell sounded, and we followed the group into a large handsome saloon hung with red silk and old tapestries, where the bride and groom sat down in chairs placed for them at the rail before the syndic's desk, with their two witnesses at their left. A clerk recorded the names and residences of all four; and then the usher summoned the syndic, who entered, a large, stout old gentleman, with a tricolor sash accenting his fat middle – waist he had none. Everybody rose, and he asked the bride and groom severally if they would help each other through life and be kind and faithful; then in a long, mechanical formula, which I could not hear, he dismissed them. They signed a register, and the affair was all over for us, and just begun for them, poor things. The bride seemed a little moved when we returned to the anteroom; she borrowed her husband's handkerchief, lightly blew her nose with it, and tucked it back in his breast-pocket.

## XXXVII.

In pursuance of an intention of studying Florence more seriously than anything here represents, I assisted one morning at a session of the police court, which I was willing to compare with the like tribunal at home. I found myself in much the same sort of crowd as frequents the police court here; but upon the whole the Florentine audience, though shabby, was not so truculent-looking nor so dirty as the Boston one; and my respectability was consoled when I found myself shoulder to shoulder with an *abbate* in it. The thing that chiefly struck me in the court itself was the abundance of form and "presence," as compared with ours. Instead of our clerk standing up in his sack-coat, the court was opened by a crier in a black gown with a white shoulder-knot, and order was kept by others as ceremoniously apparelled, instead of two fat, cravatless officers in blue flannel jackets and Japanese fans. The judges, who were three, sat on a dais under a bust of King Umberto, before desks equipped with inkstands and sand-boxes exactly like those in the theatre. Like the ushers, they wore black gowns and white shoulder-knots, and had on visorless caps bound with silver braid; the lawyers also were in gowns. The business with which the court opened seemed to be some civil question, and I waited for no other. The judges examined the witnesses, and were very keen and quick with them, but not severe; and what I admired in all was the good manner, — self-respectful, unabashed; nobody seemed browbeaten or afraid. One of the witnesses was one whom people near me called a *gobbino* (hunchbackling), and whose deformity was so grotesque that I am afraid a crowd of our people would have laughed at him, but no one smiled there. He bore himself with dignity, answering to the beautiful Florentine name of Vanuccio Vanucci; the judges first addressed him as *voi* (you), but slipped insensibly into the more respectful *lei* (lordship) before they were done with him. I was too far off from them to make out what it was all about.

## XXXVIII.

I believe there are not many crimes of violence in Florence; the people are not brutal, except to the dumb brutes, and there is probably more cutting and stabbing in Boston; as for shooting, it is almost unheard of. A society for the prevention of cruelty to animals has been established by some humane English ladies, which directs its efforts wisely to awakening sympathy for them in the children. They are taught kindness to cats and dogs, and it is hoped that when they grow up they will even be kind to horses. These poor creatures, which have been shut out of the pale of human sympathy in Italy by their failure to embrace the Christian doctrine "(*Non sono Cristiani!*"), are very harshly treated by the Florentines, I was told; though I am bound to say that I never saw an Italian beating a horse. The horses look wretchedly underfed and overworked, and doubtless they suffer from the hard, smooth pavements of the city, which are so delightful to drive on; but as for the savage scourgings, the kicking with heavy boots, the striking over the head with the butts of whips, I take leave to doubt if it is at all worse with the Italians than with us, though it is so bad with us that the sooner the Italians can be reformed the better.

If they are not very good to animals, I saw how kind they could be to the helpless and hapless of our own species, in a visit which I paid one morning to the Pia Casa di Ricovero in Florence. This refuge for pauperism was established by the first Napoleon, and is formed of two old convents, which he suppressed and joined together for the purpose. It has now nearly eight hundred inmates, men, women, and children; and any one found begging in the streets is sent there. The whole is under police government, and an officer was detailed to show me about the airy wards and sunny courts, and the clean, wholesome dormitories. The cleanliness of the place, in fact, is its most striking characteristic, and is promoted in the persons of the inmates by baths, perfunctory or voluntary, every week. The kitchen, with its shining coppers, was deliciously fragrant with the lunch preparing, as I passed through it: a mush of Indian meal boiled in a substantial meat-broth. This was served with an abundance of bread and half a gill of wine in pleasant refectories; some very old incapables and incurables were eating it in bed. The aged leisure gregariously gossiping in the wards, or blinking vacantly in the sunshine of the courts, was an enviable spectacle; and I should have liked to know what these old fellows had to complain of; for, of course, they were discontented. The younger inmates were all at work; there was an admirably appointed shop where they were artistically instructed in wood-carving and fine cabinet-work; and there were whole rooms full of little girls knitting, and of big girls weaving: all the clothes worn there are woven there. I do not know why the sight of a very old tailor in spectacles, cutting out a dozen suits of clothes at a time, from as many thicknesses of cloth, should have been so fascinating. Perhaps in his presence I was hovering upon the secret of the conjectured grief of that aged leisure: its clothes were all cut of one size and pattern!

## XXXIX.

I have spoken already of the excellent public schools of Florence, which I heard extolled again and again as the best in Italy; and I was very glad of the kindness of certain friends, which enabled me to visit them nearly all. The first which I saw was in that famous old Via de' Bardi where Romola lived, and which was inspired by a charity as large-minded

as her own. It is for the education of young girls in book-
keeping and those departments of commerce in which they
can be useful to themselves and others, and has a subsidy
from the state of two-fifths of its expenses; the girls pay each
ten francs a year for their tuition, and the rest comes from
private sources. The person who had done most to establish
it was the lady in whose charge I found it, and who was giving
her time to it for nothing; she was the wife of a professor in
the School of Superior Studies (as the University of Florence
modestly calls itself), and I hope I may be forgiven, for
the sake of the completer idea of the fact which I wish
to present, if I trench so far as to add that she found her
devotion to it consistent with all her domestic duties and
social pleasures: she had thoroughly philosophized it, and
enjoyed it practically as well as æsthetically. The school
occupies three rooms on the ground floor of an old palace,
whose rear windows look upon the Arno; and in these
rooms are taught successively writing and mathematics,
the principles of book-keeping, and practical book-keeping,
with English and French throughout the three years' course.
The teacher of penmanship was a professor in the Academy
of Fine Arts, and taught it in its principles; in this case, as
in most others, the instruction is without text-books, and
seemed to me more direct and sympathetic than ours: the
pupil felt the personal quality of the teacher. There are fifty
girls in the school, mostly from shop-keeping families, and of
all ages from twelve to seventeen, and although it had been
established only a short time, several of them had already
found places. They were prettily and tidily dressed, and
looked interested and happy. They rose when we entered
a room, and remained standing till we left it; and it was

easy to see that their mental training was based upon a habit of self-respectful subordination, which would be quite as useful hereafter. Some little infractions of discipline – I have forgotten what – were promptly rebuked by Signora G–, and her rebuke was received in the best spirit. She said she had no trouble with her girls, and she was experiencing now, at the end of the first year, the satisfaction of success in her experiment: hers I call it, because, though there is a similar school in Naples, she was the foundress of this in Florence.

There is now in Italy much inquiry as to what the Italians can best do to resume their place in the business of the world; and in giving me a letter to the director of the Popular Schools in Florence, Signora G – told me something of what certain good heads and hearts there had been thinking and doing. It appeared to these that Italy, with her lack of natural resources, could never compete with the great industrial nations in manufacturing, but they believed that she might still excel in the mechanical arts which are nearest allied to the fine arts, if an intelligent interest in them could be reawakened in her people, and they could be enlightened and educated to the appreciation of skill and beauty in these. To this end a number of Florentine gentlemen united to establish the Popular Schools, where instruction is given free every Sunday to any man or boy of any age who chooses to wash his hands and face and come. Each of these gentlemen pledges himself to teach personally in the schools, or to pay for a teacher in his place; there is no aid from the state; all is the work of private beneficence, and no one receives pay for service in the schools except the porter.

I found them in a vast old palace in the Via Parione, and the director kindly showed me through every department. Instruction is given in reading, writing, and arithmetic, and the other simpler branches; but the final purpose of the schools is to train the faculties for the practice of the decorative arts, and any art in which disciplined and nimble wits are useful. When a pupil enters, his name is registered, and his history in the school is carefully recorded up to the time he leaves it. It was most interesting to pass from one room to another, and witness the operation of the admirable ideas which animated the whole. Of course, the younger pupils were the quicker; but the director called them up without regard to age or standing, and let me hear them answer their teachers' questions, merely saying, "This one has been with us six weeks; this one, two; this one, three years," etc. They were mostly poor fellows out of the streets, but often they were peasants who walked five or six miles to and fro to profit by the chance offered them for a little life and light. Sometimes they were not too clean, and the smell in the rooms must have been trying to the teachers; but they were decently clad, attentive, and well-behaved. One of the teachers had come up through the schools, with no other training, and was very efficient. There was a gymnasium, and the pupils were taught the principles of hygiene; there was abundant scientific apparatus, and a free circulating library. There is no religious instruction, but in one of the rooms a professor from the Studii Superiori was lecturing on the Duties of a Citizen; I heard him talk to the boys about theft; he was very explicit with them, but just and kindly; from time to time he put a question to test their intelligence and attention. An admirable spirit of democracy – that is to say, of humanity and good sense – seemed to prevail throughout. The director made one little fellow read to me. Then, "What is your business?" he asked. "Cleaning out eave-troughs." Some of the rest tittered. "Why laugh?" demanded the director sternly. "It is an occupation, like another."

There are no punishments; for gross misbehavior the offender is expelled. On the other hand, the pupils are given premiums for excellence, and are encouraged to put them into the savings-bank. The whole course is for four years; but in the last years room few remained. Of these was a certain *rosso* (red-head), whom the director called up. Afterwards he told me that this *rosso* had a wild romantic passion for America, whither he supremely desired to go, and that it would be an inexpressible pleasure for him to have seen me. I came away regretting that he could form so little idea from my looks of what America was really like.

In an old Medici palace, which was also once a convent, at the Oltrarno end of the Trinità bridge, is the National Female Normal School, one of two in the kingdom, the other being at Naples. On the day of my visit, the older girls had just returned from the funeral of one of their professors, – a priest of the neighboring parish of S. Spirito. It was at noon, and, in the natural reaction, they were chatting gayly; and as they ranged up and down stairs and through the long sunny corridors, pairing off, and whispering and laughing over their luncheon, they were very much like school-girls at home. The porter sent me upstairs through their formidable ranks to the room of the professor to whom I was accredited, and he kindly showed me through his department. It was scientific, and to my ignorance, at least, was thoroughly equipped for its work with the usual apparatus; but at that moment the light, clean, airy rooms were empty of students; and he presently gave me in charge of the directress, Signora Billi, who kindly led the way through the whole establishment. Some Boston lady, whom she had met in our educational exhibit at the Exposition in Paris, had made interest with her for all future Americans by giving her a complete set of our public-school text-books, and she showed me with great satisfaction, in one of the rooms, a set of American school furniture, desks, and seats. But there the Americanism of the Normal School ended. The instruction was oral, the text-books few or none; but every student had her note-book in which she set down the facts and principles imparted. I do not know what the comparative advantages of the different systems are; but it seemed to me that there must be more life and sympathy in the Italian.

The pupils, who are of all ages from six years to twenty, are five hundred in number, and are nearly all from the middle class, though some are from the classes above and below that. They come there to be fitted for teaching, and are glad to get the places which the state, which educates them for nothing, pays scantily enough, – two hundred and fifty dollars a year at most. They were all neatly dressed, and well-mannered, of course, from the oldest to the youngest; the discipline is perfect, and the relation of teachers and pupils, I understood, most affectionate. Perhaps after saying this I ought to add that the teachers are all ladies, and young ladies. One of these was vexed that I should see her girls with their hats and sacks on: but they were little ones and just going home; the little ones were allowed to go home at one o'clock, while the others remained from nine till two. In the room of the youngest were two small Scotchwomen who had quite forgotten their parents' dialect; but in their blue eyes and auburn hair, in everything but their speech, they were utterly alien to the dusky bloom and gleaming black of the Italians about them. The girls were nearly all of the dark type, though there was here and there one of those opaque Southern blondes one finds in Italy. Fair or dark, however, they all had looks of bright intelligence, though I should say that in beauty they were below the American average. All their surroundings here were wholesome and good, and the place was thoroughly comfortable, as the Italians understand comfort. They have no fire in the coldest weather, though at Signora G—'s commercial school they had stoves, to be used in extreme cases; but on the other hand they had plenty of light and sunny air, and all the brick floors and whitewashed walls were exquisitely clean. I should not have been much the wiser for seeing them at their lessons, and I shall always be glad of that impression of hopeful, cheerful young life which the sight of their leisure gave me, as they wandered happy and free through the corridors where the nuns used to pace with downcast eyes and folded palms; and I came away very well satisfied with my century.

My content was in nowise impaired by the visit which I made to the girls' public school in Via Montebello. It corresponded, I suppose, to one of our primary schools; and here, as elsewhere, the teaching was by dictation; the children had readers, but no other text-books; these were in the hands of the teachers alone. Again everything was very clean, very orderly, very humane and kindly. The little ones in the various rooms, called up at random, were wonderfully proficient in reading, mathematics, grammar, and geography; one small person showed an intimacy with the map of Europe which was nothing less than dismaying.

I did not succeed in getting to the boys' schools, but I was told that they were practically the same as this; and it seemed to me that if I must miss either, it was better to see the future mothers of Italy at their books. Here alone was there any hint of the church in the school: it was a Friday, and the priest was coming to teach the future mothers their catechism.

## XL.

Few of my readers, I hope, have failed to feel the likeness of these broken and ineffectual sketches to the pictures in stone which glare at you from the windows of the mosaicists on the Lungarno and in the Via Borgognissanti; the wonder of them is greater than the pleasure. I have myself had the fancy, in my work, of a number of small views and figures of mosaic, set in a slab of black marble for a table-top, or – if the reader does not like me to be so ambitious – a paper-weight; and now I am tempted to form a border to this *capo d'opera*, bizarre and irregular, such as I have sometimes seen composed of the bits of *pietra viva* left over from a larger work. They are mere fragments of color, scraps and shreds of Florence, which I find still gleaming more or less dimly in my note-books, and I have no notion of making any ordered arrangement of them.

But I am sure that if I shall but speak of how the sunshine lies in the Piazza of the Annunziata at noonday, falling on the feebly dribbling grotesques of the fountain there, and on John of Bologna's equestrian grand duke, and on that dear and ever lovely band of babes by Luca della Robbia in the façade of the Hospital of the Innocents, I shall do enough to bring it all back to him who has once seen it, and to justify myself at least in his eyes.

The beautiful pulpit of Donatello in San Lorenzo I find associated in sensation with the effect, from the old cloistered court of that church, of Brunelleschi's dome and Giotto's tower showing in the pale evening air above all the picturesque roofs between San Lorenzo and the cathedral; and not remote from these is my pleasure in the rich vulgarity and affluent bad taste of the modern decoration of the *Caffè del Parlatnmto*, in which one takes one's ice under the china of all these pretty girls, popping their little sculp tured heads out of the lunettes below the frieze, with the hats and bonnets of fifteen years ago on them.

Do you remember, beloved brethren and sisters of Florentine sojourn, the little windows beside the grand portals of the palaces, the *cantine*, where you could buy a graceful wicker-covered flask of the prince's or marquis's wine? "Open from ten till four – till one on holidays," they were lettered; and in the Borgo degli Albizzi I saw the Cantina Filicaja, though it had no longer the old sigh for Italy upon its lips: –

"Deh, fossi tu men bella o almen più forte!"

I am far from disdaining the memory of my horse-car tour of the city, on the track which followed so nearly the line of the old city wall that it showed me most of the gates still left standing, and the last grand duke's arch of triumph, very brave in the sunset light. The tramways make all the long distances in the Florentine outskirts and suburbs, and the cars never come when you want them, just as with us, and are always as crowded.

I had a great deal of comfort in two old fellows, unoccupied custodians, in the convent of San Marco, who, while we were all fidgeting about, doing our Fra Angelico or our Savonarola, sat motionless in a patch of sunshine and tranquilly gossipped together in senile falsetto. On the other hand, I never saw truer grief, or more of it, in a custodian than the polite soul displayed in the Bargello on whom we came so near the hour of closing one day that he could show us almost nothing. I could see that it wrung his heart that we should have paid our francs to come in then, when the Dante in the peaceful Giotto fresco was only a pensive blur to the eye, and the hideous realizations of the great Pest in wax were mere indistinguishable nightmares. We tried to console him by assuring him of our delight in Della Robbia's singing boys in another room, and of the compensation we had in getting away from the Twelve (Useless) Labors of Hercules by Rossi, and two or three particularly unpleasant muscular Abstractions of Michael Angelo. It was in fact too dark to see much of the museum, and we had to come again for that; but no hour could have been better than that of the falling dusk for the old court, with its beautiful staircase, where so many hearts had broken in the anguish of death, and so many bloody heads rolled upon the insensible stones since the first Podestà of Florence had made the Bargello his home, till the last Medici had made it his prison.

Of statues and of pictures I have spoken very little, because it seems to me that others have spoken more than enough. Yet I have hinted that I did my share both of suffering and enjoying in galleries and churches, and I have here and there still lurking in my consciousness a color, a look, a light, a line from some masterpiece of Botticelli, of Donatello, of Mino da Fiesole, which I would fain hope will be a consolation forever, but which I will not vainly attempt to impart to others. I will rather beg the reader when he goes to Florence, to go for my sake, as well as his own, to the Academy and look at the Spring of Botticelli as long and often as he can keep away from the tender and dignified and exquisitely refined Mino da Fiesole sculptures in the Badia, or wherever else he may find them. These works he may enjoy without technique, and simply upon condition of his being a tolerably genuine human creature. There is something also very sweet and winningly simple in the archaic reliefs in the base of Giotto's tower; and the lessee of the Teatro Umberto in showing me behind the scenes of his theatre had a politeness that was delicious, and comparable to nothing less than the finest works of art.

In quality of courtesy the Italians are still easily first of all men, as they are in most other things when they will, though I am not sure that the old gentleman who is known in Florence as The American, *par excellence*, is not perhaps pre-eminent in the art of driving a circus-chariot. This compatriot has been one of the most striking and characteristic features of the place for a quarter of a century, with his team of sixteen or twenty horses guided through the Florentine streets by the reins gathered into his hands. From time to time his horses have run away and smashed his carriage, or at least pulled him from his seat, so that now he has himself strapped to the box, and four grooms sit with folded arms on the seats behind him, ready to jump down and fly at the horses' heads. As the strange figure, drawn at a slow trot, passes along, with stiffly waxed mustache and impassive face, it looks rather like a mechanical contrivance in the human form; and you are yielding to this fancy, when, approaching a corner, it breaks into a long cry, astonishingly harsh and fierce, to warn people in the next street of its approach. It is a curious sight, and seems to belong to the time when rich and privileged people used their pleasure to be eccentric, and the "madness" of Englishmen especially was the amazement and delight of the Continent. It is in character with this that the poor old gentleman should bear one of our own briefly historical names, and that he should illustrate in the indulgence of his caprice the fact that no great length of time is required to arrive at all that centuries can do for a noble family. I have been sorry to observe a growing impatience with him on the part of the Florentine journalists. Upon the occasion of his last accident they asked if it was not time his progresses should be forbidden. Next to tearing down the Ponte Vecchio, I can imagine nothing worse.

Journalism is very active in Florence, and newspapers are sold and read everywhere; they are conspicuous in the hands of people who are not supposed to read; and more than once the cab-driver whom I called at a street corner had to fold up his cheap paper and put it away before he could respond. They are of a varying quality. The "Nazione," which is serious and political, is as solidly, if not so heavily, written as an English journal; the "Fanfulla della Domenica'" which is literary, contains careful and brilliant reviews of new books. The cheap papers are apt to be inflammatory in politics; if humorous, they are local and somewhat unintelligible. The more pretentious satirical papers are upon the model of the

French, — a little more political, but abounding mostly in jokes at the expense of the seventh commandment, which the Latins find so droll. There are in all thirty periodicals, monthly, weekly, and daily, published in Florence, which you are continually assured is no longer the literary centre of Italy. It is true none of the leaders of the new realistic movement in fiction are Florentines by birth or residence; the chief Italian poet, Carducci, lives in Bologna, the famous traveller De Amicis lives in Turin, and most new books are published at Milan or Naples. But I recur again to the group of accomplished scholars who form the intellectual body of the Studii Superiori, or University of Florence; and thinking of such an able and delightful historian as Villari, and such a thorough and indefatigable littérateur as Gubernatis, whom the congenial intellectual atmosphere of Florence has attracted from Naples and Piedmont, I should not, if I were a Florentine, yield the palm without a struggle.

One does not turn one's face from Florence without having paid due honors in many a regretful, grateful look to the noble and famous river that runs through her heart. You are always coming upon the Arno, and always seeing it in some new phase or mood. Belted with its many bridges, and margined with towers and palaces, it is the most beautiful and stately thing in the beautiful and stately city, whether it is in a dramatic passion from the recent rains, or dreamily raving of summer drouth over its dam, and stretching a bar of silver from shore to shore. The tawny splendor of its flood; the rush of its rapids; the glassy expanses in which the skies mirror themselves by day, and the lamps by night; the sweeping curve of the pale buff line of houses that follows its course, — give a fascination which is not lost even when

the anxiety of a threatened inundation mingles with it. The
storms of a single night, sending down their torrents from
the hills, set it foaming; it rises momently, and nothing but
the presence of all the fire-engine companies in the city
allays public apprehension. What they are to do to the Arno
in case it overflows its banks, or whether they are similarly
called out in summer when it shrinks to a rill in its bed, and
sends up clouds of mosquitoes, I do not know; nor am I quite
comfortable in thinking the city is drained into it. From the
vile old rancid stenches which steam up from the crevices
in the pavement everywhere, one would think the city was
not drained at all; but this would be as great a mistake
as to think New York is not cleaned, merely because it
looks filthy.

Before we left Florence we saw the winter drowse broken
in the drives and alleys of the Cascine; we saw the grass,
green from November till April, snowed with daisies, and
the floors of the dusky little dingles empurpled with violets.
The nightingales sang from the poplar tops in the dull rich
warmth; the carriages blossomed with lovely hats and parasols; handsome cavaliers and slim-waisted ladies dashed by
on blooded horses (I will say blooded for the effect), and
a fat flower-girl urged her wares upon every one she could
overtake. It is enough to suggest what the Cascine could
be to Florence in the summer, and enough to make one
regret the winter, when one could have it nearly all to one's
self.

You can never see the Boboli Garden with the same
sense of ownership, for it distinctly belongs to the king's
palace, and the public has the range of it only on Sundays,
when the people throng it. But, unless one is very greedy,

it is none the less a pleasure for that, with its charming, silly grottos, its masses of ivy-covered wall, its curtains of laurel-hedge, its black spires of cypress and domes of pine, its weather-beaten marbles, its sad, unkempt lawns, its grotesque, overgrown fountain, with those sea-horses so much too big for its lake, its wandering alleys and moss-grown seats abounding in talking age and whispering lovers. It has a tangled vastness in which an American might almost lose his self-consciousness; and the view of Florence from one of its heights is incomparably enchanting, – like every other view of Florence.

Like that, for instance, which one has from the tower of the Palazzo Vecchio, looking down on the picturesque surfaces of the city tiles, the silver breadth and stretch of the Arno, the olive and vine clad hills, the vast champaign widening in the distance till the misty tops of the mountains softly close it in at last. Here, as from San Miniato, the domed and galleried bulk of the cathedral showed prodigiously first of all things; then the eye rested again and again upon the lowered crests of the mediæval towers, monumentally abounding among the modern roofs that swelled above their broken pride. The Florence that I saw was indeed no longer the Florence of the sentimentalist's feeble desire, or the romancer's dream, but something vastly better: contemporary, real, busy in its fashion, and wholesomely and every-daily beautiful. And my heart still warms to the famous town, not because of that past which, however heroic and aspiring, was so wrong-headed and bloody and pitiless, but because of the present, safe, free, kindly, full of possibilities of prosperity and fraternity, like that of Boston or Denver.

The weather had grown suddenly warm overnight. I looked again at the distant mountains, where they smouldered along the horizon: they were purple to their tips, and no ghost of snow glimmered under any fold of their mist. Our winter in Florence had come to an end.

# Panforte Di Siena

Month out of our winter at Florence we gave to Siena, whither we went early in February. At that time there were no more signs of spring in the landscape than there were in December, except for here and there an almond-tree, which in the pale pink of its thronging blossoms showed delicately as a lady's complexion in the unfriendly air. The fields were in their green arrest, but the trees were bare, and the yellow river that wandered along beside the railroad looked sullen and cold under the dun sky.

After we left the Florentine plain, we ran between lines of reddish hills, sometimes thickly wooded, sometimes showing on their crests only the stems and tops of scattering pines and poplars, such as the Tuscan painters were fond of putting into their Judean backgrounds. There were few tokens of life in the picture; we saw some old women tending sheep and spinning with their distaffs in the pastures; and in the distance there were villages cropping out of the hill-tops and straggling a little way down the slopes. At times we whirled by the ruins of a castle, and nearer Siena

we caught sight of two or three walled towers which had
come down from the Middle Ages apparently with every
turret in repair. Our course was south-westward, but we
were continually mounting into the cold, thin air of the volcanic hill-country, at the summit of which the old Ghibelline
city still sits capital, proud of her past, beautiful and noble
even among Italian towns, and wearing in her mural crown
the cathedral second in splendor and surprise only to the
jewel-church in the belt of Venice.

It is not my habit to write such fine rhetoric as this,
the reader will bear me witness; and I suspect that it is a
prophetic tint from an historical sketch of Siena, to which,
after ascertaining the monotony of the landscape, I could
dedicate the leisure of our journey with a good conscience.
It forms part of "La Nuova Guida di Siena," and it grieves
me that the titlepage of my copy should have been lost,
so that I cannot give the name of an author whose eloquence I delight in. He says: "Siena is lifted upon hills that
rise alluring and delicious in the centre of Tuscany. . . . Its
climate is soft, temperate, and wholesome. The summer
sojourn is very grateful there on account of the elevated
position and the sea breezes that, with an agreeable con-
stancy, prevail in that season. . . . The panorama of the city
is something enchanting. . . . Every step reveals startling
changes of perspective, now lovely, now stern, but always
stamped with a physiognomy of their own, a characteristic
originality. From all points is seen the slim, proud tower
of the Mangia, that lifts among the clouds its battlemented
crest, its arrowy and exquisite shaft. Viewed from the top
of this tower, Siena presents the figure of a star, — a figure
formed by the diverse rays or lines of its streets traced upon

the shoulder of the hills. The loveliest blue of the most lovely Italian sky irradiates our city with the purest light, in which horizons magnificent and vast open upon the eye. . . . The hills and the plain are everywhere clothed with rich olive groves, festive orchards, luxuriant vineyards, and delightful bosks of oak, of chestnut, and of walnut, which form the umbrageous breathing-places of the enchanting landscape, and render the air pure and oxygenated. "The native inhabitants of this paradise are entirely worthy of it. "No people in Italy, except, perhaps, the Neapolitans, has the wide-awake-mindedness, the liveliness of character, the quickness of spirit, the keen-witted joyousness of the Sienese. . . . The women dress modestly, but with taste. They are gracious, amiable, inclined to amusement, and affectionate in their families. In general their honesty gives no ground for jealousy to their husbands; they are extremely refined in manner, and renowned for their grace and beauty. The comeliness of their figures, the regularity of their lineaments, as well as their vivid coloring, which reveals in them an enviable freshness of fibre and good blood purified by the mountain air, justly awaken the admiration of strangers. . . . In the women and the men alike exist the sweetness of pronunciation, the elegance of phrase, and the soft clearness of the true Tuscan accent. . . . Hospitality and the cordial reception of strangers are the hereditary, the proverbial virtues of the Sienese. . . . The pride of the Sienese character is equal to its hospitality; and this does not spring from roughness of manners and customs, but is a noble pride, magnanimous, worthy of an enlightened people with a self-derived dignity, and intensely attached to its own liberty and independence. The Sienese, whom one historian has called the French of Italy, are ardent spirits, enthusiastic, resolute, energetic, courageous, and prompt beyond any other people to brandish their arms in defence of their country. They have a martial nature, a fervid fancy, a lively imagination; they are born artists; laborious, affable, affectionate, expansive; they are frank and loyal friends, but impressionable, impetuous, fiery to exaltation. Quick to anger, they are ready to forgive, which shows their excellence of heart. They are polite, but unaffected. Another trait of their gay and sympathetic character is their love of song, of the dance, and of all gymnastic exercises. . . . Dante called the Sienese *gente vana* (a vain people). But we must reflect that the *altissimo poeta* was a Florentine, and though a sublime genius, he was not able to emancipate himself from that party hate and municipal rivalry, the great curse of his time."

But for that final touch about Dante, I might have thought I was reading a description of the Americans, and more especially the Bostonians, so exactly did my author's eulogy of the Sienese embody the facts of our own character. But that touch disillusioned me: even Dante would not have called the Bostoniane *gente vana*, unless he had proposed to spend the rest of his life in London. As it was, I was impatient to breathe that wondrous air, to bask in that light, to behold that incomparable loveliness, to experience that proverbial hospitality and that frank and loyal friendship, to mingle in the song and dance and the gymnastic exercises; and nothing but the sober-minded deliberation of the omnibus-train which was four hours in going to Siena, prevented me from throwing myself into the welcoming embrace of the cordial city at once.

## II.

I had time not only to reflect that perhaps Siena distinguished between strangers arriving at her gates, and did not bestow an indiscriminate hospitality, but to wander back with the "New Guide" quite to the dawn of her history, when Senio, the son of Remus, flying from the wrath of his uncle Romulus, stopped where Siena now stands and built himself a castle. Whether the city got her name from Senio or not, it is certain that she adopted the family arms; and to this day the she-wolf suckling the twins is as much blazoned about Siena as about Rome, if not more. She was called Urbs Lupata even by the Romans, from the wolf-bearing seal of her chief magistrate; and a noble Roman family sent one of its sons as early as 303 to perish at Siena for the conversion of the city to Christianity. When the empire fell, Siena suffered less than the other Tuscan cities from the barbarian incursions; but she came under the rule of the Longobard kings, and then was one of the "free cities" of Charlemagne, from whose counts and barons, enriched by his gifts of Sienese lands and castles, the Sienese nobility trace their descent. These foreign robbers, whose nests the Florentines went out of their gates to destroy, in their neighborhood, voluntarily left their castles in the Sienese territory, and came into the city, which they united with the bishops in embellishing with beautiful palaces and ruling with an iron hand, till the commons rose and made good their claim to a share in their own government. Immunities and privileges were granted by Cæsar and Peter, and at the close of the twelfth century a republican government, with an elective magistracy, was fully developed, and the democratized city entered upon a career of great material prosperity. "But in the midst of this potent activity of political and commercial life, Siena more than any other Italian city was afflicted with municipal rivalries and intestine discords. To-day the nobles triumphed and hurled the commons from power; to-morrow the people took a bloody revenge and banished every patrician from the city. Every change of administration was accompanied by ostracism, by violence, by public tumults, by continual upheavals;" and these feuds of families, of parties, and of classes were fostered and perpetuated by the warring ambitions of the popes and emperors. From the first, Siena was Ghibelline and for the emperors, and it is odd that one of her proudest victories should have been won against Henry the son of Barbarossa. When that emperor threatened the free cities with ruin, Siena was the only one in Tuscany that shut her gates against him; and when Henry laid siege to her, her people sallied out of Fontebranda and San Marco, and fell upon his Germans and put them to flight.

The Florentines, as we have seen, were of the pope's politics; or, rather, they were for their own freedom, which they thought his politics favored, and the Sienese were for theirs, which they believed the imperial success would establish. They never could meet upon the common ground of their common love of liberty, but kept battling on through four centuries of miserable wars till both were enslaved. Siena had her shameful triumph when she helped in the great siege that restored the Medici to Florence in 1530, and Florence had her cruel revenge when her tyrant Cosimo I. entered Siena at the head of the imperial forces fifteen years later. The Florentines met their first great defeat at the hands of the Sienese and of their own Ghibelline exiles at Montaperto (twelve miles from Siena) in 1260, when the slaughter was so great, as Dante says, "che fece l'Arbia colorata in rosso;" and in 1269 the Sienese were routed by their own Guelph exiles and the Florentines at Colle di Val d'Elsa.

A story is told of an official of Siena to whom the Florentines sent in 1860 to invite his fellow-citizens to join them in celebrating the union of Tuscany with the kingdom of Italy. He said, Yes, they would be glad to send a deputation of Sienese to Florence, but would the Florentines really like to have them come? "Surely! Why not?" "Oh, that affair of Montaperto, you know," – as if it were of the year before, and must still, after six hundred years, have been rankling in the Florentine mind. But perhaps in that time it had become confused there with other injuries, or perhaps the Florentines of 1860 felt that they had sufficiently avenged themselves by their victory of 1269. This resulted in the triumph of the Guelphs in Siena, and finally in the substitution of the magistracy of the Nine for that of the Thirty. These Nine, or the Noveschi, ruled the city for two hundred and fifty years with such unscrupulous tyranny and infamous corruption that they "succeeded in destroying every generous sentiment, in sapping the noble pride of character in the Sienese population, and if not in extinguishing, at least in cooling, their ardent love of liberty," and preparing them for the rule of the everdreaded one-man power, which appeared in the person of Pandolfo Petrucci in 1487. He misruled Siena for twenty-five years, playing there, with less astuteness and greater ferocity, the part which Lorenzo de' Medici had played a century earlier in earlier rotten Florence. Petrucci, too, like Lorenzo, was called the Magnificent, and he, too, passed his life in sensual debauchery, in political intrigues ending in bloody revenges and reprisals, and in the protection of the arts, letters, and religion. Of course he beautified the city, and built palaces, churches, and convents with the money he stole from the people whom he gave peace to prosper in. He, too, died tranquilly of his sins and excesses, his soul reeking with treasons and murders like the fascinating Lorenzo's; and his sons tried to succeed him like Lorenzo's, but were deposed like Pietro de' Medici and banished. One of his pleasing family was that Achille Petrucci who, in the massacre of St. Bartholomew at Paris, cut the throat of the great Protestant admiral, Coligny.

After them, the Sienese enjoyed a stormy and intermittent liberty within and varying fortunes of war without, till the Emperor Charles V, having subdued Florence, sent a Spanish garrison to Siena with orders to build him a fort in that city. The Spaniards were under the command of Don Hurtado de Mendoza, who was not only, as my "New Guide" describes him, "ex-monk, astute, subtle, fascinating in address, profound dissimulator," but also the author of the "History of the War of Granada," and of one of the most delightful books in the world, namely, "The Life of Lazarillo de Tormes," Spanish rogue and beggar, for whose sake I freely forgive him on my part all his sins against the Sienese; especially as they presently drove him and his Spaniards out of the city and demolished his fort.

The Sienese had regained their freedom, but they could hope to keep it only by the help of the French and their allies the Florentine exiles, who were plotting under the Strozzi against the Medici. The French friendship came to little or nothing but promises, the exiles were few and feeble, and in 1554 the troops of the Emperor and of Duke Cosimo – him of the terrible face and the blood-stained soul, murderer of his son, and father of a family of adulteresses and assassins – came and laid siege to the doomed city. The siege lasted eighteen months, and until the Sienese were wasted by famine and pestilence, and the women fought beside the men for the city which was their country and the last hope of liberty in Italy. When the famine began they drove out the *useless mouths* (*bocche inutili*), the old men and women and the orphan children, hoping that the enemy would have pity on these hapless creatures; the Spaniards massacred most of them before their eyes. Fifteen hundred peasants, who tried to bring food into the city, were hung before the walls on the trees, which a Spanish writer says "seemed to bear dead men." The country round about was laid waste; a hundred thousand of its inhabitants perished, and the fields they had tilled lapsed into pestilential marshes breathing fever and death. The inhabitants of the city were reduced from forty to six thousand; seven hundred families preferred exile to slavery.

Charles V. gave Siena as a fief to his son, Philip II, who ceded it to Cosimo I, and he built there the fort which the Spaniards had attempted. It remained under the good Lorrainese dukes till Napoleon made it capital of his Department of the Ombrone, and it returned to them at his fall. In 1860 it was the first Tuscan city to vote for the union of Italy

under Victor Emmanuel, — the only honest king known to
history, says my "New Guida."


### III.

It is a "New Guide" full of the new wine of our epoch, and
it brags not only of the warriors, the saints, the popes, the
artists, the authors, who have illustrated the Sienese name,
but of the two great thinkers in religion and politics who
have given her truer glory. The bold pontiff Alexander III.,
who put his foot on the neck of the Emperor at Venice, was
a Sienese; the meek, courageous St. Catherine, daughter of
a dyer, and the envoy of popes and princes, was a Sienese;
Sallustio Bandini, the inventor of the principle of Free Trade
in commerce, was a Sienese; and Socinus, the inventor of
Free Thought in religion, was a Sienese. There is a statue
to Bandini in one of the chief places of Siena, but when my
"New Guide" was written there was as yet no memorial of
Socinus. "The fame of this glorious apostle," he cries bitterly,
"who has been called the father of modern rationalism, is
cherished in England, in France, in Italy, in Switzerland, in
Holland, in Poland, in America. Only Siena, who should
remember with noble pride her most illustrious son, has
no street named for him, no bust, no stone. Rightly do the
strangers who visit our city marvel at neglect which denies
him even a commemorative tablet in the house where he
was born, — the Casa Sozzini, now Palazzo Malavolta, 21 Via
Ricasoli." The justness of this censure is not impugned by
the fact that the tablet has since been placed there; perhaps it
was the scorn of my "New Guide" which lashed the Sienese
to the act of tardy recognition. This has now found stately

utterance in the monumental Italian which is the admiration
and despair of other languages: —

"In the first Half of the 16th Century
Were born in this House
Lelio and Fausto Sozzini,
Scholars, Philosophers, Philanthropists.
Strenuous Champions of the Liberty of Thought,
Defenders of Human Reason against the Supernatural,
They founded the celebrated Socinian School,
Forecasting by three Centuries
The doctrine of Modern Rationalism.
The Sienese Liberals, Admiring, Reverent,
Placed this Memorial.
1877."

I wandered into the court of the old palace, now involun-
tarily pea-green with mould and damp, and looked out from
the bow-shaped terrace bulging over the garden behind, and
across the olive orchards — But I forgot that I was not yet in
Siena.


## IV.

Before out arrival I had time to read all the "New Guide" had
to say about the present condition of this city. What it was
socially, morally, and personally I knew already, and what it
was industrially and commercially I learned with regret. The
prosperity of Siena had reached its height in the thirteenth
century, just before the great pest appeared. Her people
then numbered a hundred thousand from which they were
reduced by the plague to twenty thousand. Whole districts
were depopulated within the walls; the houses fell down,

the streets vanished, and the plough passed over the ruins; wide gardens, olive orchards, and vineyards still flourish where traffic was busy and life was abundant. The "New Guide" does not say so, but it is true that Siena never fully recovered from this terrible stroke. At the time of the great siege, two hundred years after the time of the great pest, she counted only forty thousand souls within her gates, and her silk and woollen industries, which still exist, were vastly shrunken from their old proportions. The most evident industry in Siena now is that of the tanners, which hangs its banners of leather from all the roofs in the famous region of Fontebranda, and envelops the birthplace of St. Catherine in an odor of tan-bark. There is also a prosperous fabric of iron furniture, principally bedsteads, which is noted throughout Italy; this, with some cotton-factories and carpet-looms on a small scale, and some agricultural implement works, is nearly all that the "New Guide" can boast, till he comes to speak of the ancient marchpane of Siena, now called Panforte, whose honored name I have ventured to bestow upon these haphazard sketches of its native city, rather because of their chance and random associations of material and decorative character than because of any rivalry in quality to which they can pretend. I often saw the panforte in shop-windows at Florence, and had the best intention in the world to test its excellence, but to this day I know only of its merits from my "New Guide." "This specialty, wholly Sienese, enjoys, in the article of sweetmeats, the primacy in Italy and beyond, and forms one of the principal branches of our industry. The panforte of Siena fears no competition or comparison, either for the exquisiteness of its flavor or for the beauty of its artistic confection: its brown paste, gemmed with broken almonds, is covered in the *panfortes de luxe* with a frosting of sugar, adorned with broideries, with laces, with flowers, with leaves, with elegant figures in lively colors, and with artistic designs, representing usually some monument of the city."

### V.

It was about dark when we reached Siena, looking down over her wall upon the station in the valley; but there was still light enough to give us proof, in the splendid quarrel of two railway porters over our baggage, of that quickness to anger and readiness to forgive which demonstrates the excellence of heart in the Sienese. These admirable types of the local character jumped furiously up and down in front of each other, and then, without striking a blow, instantly exchanged forgiveness and joined in a fraternal conspiracy to get too much money out of me for handling my trunks. I willingly became a party to their plot myself in gratitude for the impassioned spectacle they had afforded me; and I drove up through the steeply winding streets of the town with a sense of nearness to the Middle Ages not excelled even in my first visit to Quebec. Of Quebec I still think when I think of Siena; and there are many superficial points of likeness in the two cities. Each, as Dante said of one, "torregia e siede" ("sits and towers" is no bad phrase) on a mighty front of rock, round whose precipitous slopes she belts her girdling wall. The streets within wander hither and thither at will; in both they are narrow and hemmed in with the gray façades of the stone houses; without spreads a mighty valley, – watered at Quebec with the confluent St. Lawrence and St. Charles,

and walled at the horizon with primevally wooded hills;
dry at Siena with almost volcanic drought, and shut in at
the same far range by arid and sterile tops bare as the skies
above them, yet having still the same grandeur and nobility
of form. After that there is all the difference you will, – the
difference of the North and South, the difference of the Old
World and the New.

I have always been a friend of the picturesqueness of
the Cathedral Place at Quebec, and faithful to it in much
scribbling hitherto, but nothing – not even the love of
pushing a parallel – shall make me pretend that it is in
any manner or degree comparable to the old and deeply
memoried Piazza Vittorio Emmanuele at Siena. This was
anciently Piazza del Campo, but now they call it Piazza
Vittorio Emmanuele, because, since the Unification, they
want some piazza of that dear name in every Italian city, as I
have already noted; and I walked to it through the Via Cavour
which they must also have, and how it was I failed to traverse
a Via Garibaldi I do not understand. It was in the clearness
that follows the twilight when, after the sudden descent of a
vaulted passage, I stood in the piazza and saw the Tower of
the Mangia leap like a rocket into the starlit air. After all, that
does not say it: you must suppose a perfect silence, through
which this exquisite shaft forever soars. When once you have
seen the Mangia, all other towers, obelisks, and columns
are tame and vulgar and earth-rooted; that seems to quit the
ground, to be not a monument but a flight. The crescent
of the young moon, at half its height, looked sparely over
the battlements of the Palazzo Communale, from which the
tower sprang, upon the fronts of the beautiful old palaces
whose semicircle encloses the grand space before it, and

touched with its silver the waters of the loveliest fountain in the world whose statues and bas-reliefs darkled above and around a silent pool. There were shops in the basements of some of the palaces, and there were lamps around the piazza, but there seemed no one in it but ourselves, and no figure broke the gentle slope in which the ground shelves from three sides towards the Palazzo Communale, where I left the old republic in full possession when I went home through the thronged and cheerful streets to bed.

I observed in the morning that the present Italian Government had taken occasion overnight to displace the ancient Sienese signory, and had posted a sentry at the palace door. There had also sprung up a picturesque cluster of wooden-roofed market-booths where peasant women sat before heaps of fruit and vegetables, and there was a not very impressive show of butter, eggs, and poultry. Now I saw that the brick-paved slope of the piazza was moss-grown in disuse, and that the noble Gothic and Renaissance palaces seemed half of them uninhabited. But there was nothing dilapidated, nothing ruinous in the place; it had simply a forsaken look, which the feeble stir of buying and selling at the market-booths scarcely affected. The old Palace of the Commonwealth stood serene in the morning light, and its Gothic windows gazed tranquilly upon the shallow cup before it, as empty now of the furious passions, the mediæval hates and rivalries and ambitions, as of the other volcanic fires which are said once to have burned there. These, indeed, still smoulder beneath Siena, and every August a tremor of earthquake runs through her aged frame; but the heart of her fierce, free youth is at peace forevermore.

## VI.

We waited at the hotel forty-eight hours for the proverbially
cordial reception of strangers which the "New Guide" had
boasted in his Sienese. Then, as no deputation of citizens
came to offer us the hospitality of the city, we set about
finding a lodging for ourselves. At this distance of time I am
a little at a loss to know how our search, before it ended,
had involved the complicity of a *valet de place*; a short, fat,
amiable man of no definite occupation; a barber; a dealer
in bricabrac; a hunchbackling; a mysterious *facchino*; and a
were-wolf. I only know that all these were actually the agents
of our domiciliation, and that without their intervention I do
not see how we could ever have been settled in Siena. The
valet had come to show us the city, and no caricature of him
could give a sufficient impression of his forlorn and anxious
little face, his livid silk hat, his threadbare coat, his meagre
body, and his evanescent legs. He was a terribly pathetic
figure, and I count it no merit to have employed him at
once. The first day I gave him three francs to keep away,
and went myself in search of a carriage to drive us about in
search of rooms. There were no carriages at the stand, but
an old man who kept a bookstore let the lady of the party
have his chair and his *scaldino* while I went to the stable for
one. There my purpose somehow became known, and when
the driver mounted the box, and I stepped inside, the were-
wolf mounted with him, and all that morning he directed our
movements with lupine persistence and ferocity, but with a
wolfishly characteristic lack of intelligence. He had an awful
face, poor fellow, but I suspect that his ravenous eyes, his
gaunt cheeks, his shaggy hair, and his lurking, illusive looks,

were the worst of him; and heaven knows what dire need of devouring strangers he may have had. He did us no harm beyond wasting our time upon unfurnished lodgings in spite of our repeated groans and cries for furnished ones. From time to time I stopped the carriage and drove him down from the box; then he ran beside us on the pavement, and when we came to a walk on some uphill street he mounted again beside the driver, whom he at last persuaded to take us to a low tavern darkling in a sunless alley. There we finally threw off his malign spell, and driving back to our hotel, I found the little *valet de place* on the outlook. He hopefully laid hold of me, and walked me off to one impossible apartment after another, – brick-floored, scantily rugged, stoveless, husk-matressed, mountain-bedsteaded, where we should have to find our own service, and subsist mainly upon the view from the windows. This was always fine; the valet had a cultivated eye for a prospect, and there was one of these lodgings which I should have liked to take for the sake of the boys playing *mora* in the old palace court, and the old lady with a single tooth rising like an obelisk from her lower jaw, who wished to let it.

A boarding-house, or *pension*, whose windows commanded an enchanting panorama of the Sienese hills, was provided with rather too much of the landscape in-doors; and at another, which was cleanly and attractive, two obdurate young Englishmen were occupying the sunny rooms we wanted and would not vacate them for several days. The landlord conveyed a vivid impression of the violent character of these young men by whispering to me behind his hand, while he gently tried their door to see whether they were in or not, before he ventured to show me their

apartment. We could not wait, and then he tried to get
rooms for us on the floor above, in an apartment belonging
to a priest, so that we might at least eat at his table; but
he failed in this, and we resumed our search for shelter. It
must have been about this time that the short fat man appeared on the scene, and lured us off to see an apartment so
exquisitely unsuitable that he saw the despair and reproach
in our eyes, and, without giving us time to speak, promised
us a perfect apartment for the morrow, and vanished round
the first corner when we got into the street. In the very next
barber's window, however, was a notice of rooms to let,
and the barber left a lathered customer in his chair while
he ran across the way to get the keys from a shoemaker.
The shoemaker was at dinner, and his shop was shut; and
the barber having, with however great regret, to go back
to the customer left steeping in his lather, we fell into the
hands of the most sympathetic of all bricabrac dealers, who
sent us to the apartment of a French lady, – an apartment
with a northern exposure as sunless as fireless, from which
we retreated with the vague praises and promises of people
swearing in their hearts never to be caught in *that* place
again. The day went on in this vain quest, but as I returned
to the hotel at dusk I was stopped on the stairs by a mysterious *facchino* in a blouse; he had been waiting there for me,
and he whispered that the priest, whose rooms the keeper
of the pension had tried to get, now had an apartment for
me. It proved that he had not quite this, when I went to
visit him after dinner, but he had certain rooms, and a lady
occupying an apartment on the same floor had certain others; and with these and one more room which we got in the
pension below, we really sheltered ourselves at last. It was

not quite a realization of the hereditary Sienese hospitality, but we paid almost nothing for very comfortable quarters; and I do not see how a party of five could be better housed and fed for twenty-five francs a day in the world.

We must have been almost the first lodgers whom our good ecclesiastic and his niece had ever had, thru enterprise being so new; the rooms were pretty and fresh, and there was a comfortable stove in our little parlor — a *franklinetto* which, three days out of four, did not smoke — and a large kerosene lamp for our table included in the price of two francs a day which we paid for our two rooms. We grieved a good deal that we could not get all our rooms of Don A., and he sorrowed with us, showing us a jewel (*giojello*) of a room which he would have been so glad to give us if it were not already occupied by a young man of fashion and his dog. As we stood looking at it, with its stove in the corner, its carpet, its chest of drawers, and its other splendors, the good Don A. holding his three-beaked classic lamp up for us to see better, and his niece behind him lost in a passion of sympathy, which continually escaped in tender Ohs and Ahs, we sighed again, "Yes, if we could only have this, too!"

Don A. nodded his head and compressed his lips. "It would be a big thing!" (*"Sarebbe un'affarone!"*) And then we all cast our eyes to heaven, and were about to break into a common sigh, when we heard the key of the young man of fashion in the outer door; upon which, like a party of guilty conspirators, we shrank breathlessly together for a moment, and then fled precipitately into our own rooms. We parted for that night with many whispered vows of esteem, and we returned in the morning to take possession. It was in character with the whole affair that on the way we should be met by the hunchbackling (whom I find described also in my notes as a wry-necked lamb, probably from some forcible contrast which he presented to the were-wolf) with a perfectly superb apartment, full of sun, in the Piazza Vittorio Emmanuele, looking squarely upon the Palazzo Communale and the Tower of the Mangia. I was forced to confess that I had engaged my rooms.

"A pity for *you!*" cried the hunchbackling, passionately.

"I have promised," I faltered. "One must keep one's promises, no?"

"Oh, you are right, you are right," said the hunchbackling, and vanished, and I never saw him more. Had he really the apartment to which he pretended?

## VII.

No more, probably, than I had the virtue which I affected about keeping my promises. But I have never been sorry that I remained true to the word I had given Don A., and I do not see what harm there can be in saying that he was an ex-monk of the suppressed convent of Monte Olivetto, who was eking out the small stipend he received for his priestly offices in the next parish church by letting these lodgings. All the monks of Monte Olivetto had to be of noble family, and in one of our rooms the blessed candle and crucifix which hung on one side of the bed were balanced by the blazon of our host's arms in a frame on the other. Yet he was not above doing any sort of homely office for our comfort and convenience; I saw him with his priest's gown off, in his shirt-sleeves and knee-breeches, putting up a bedstead; sometimes I met him on the stairs with a load of fire-wood in his arms, which I suspect he must have been sawing in the cellar. He bowed to me over it with unabashed courtesy, and he and Maddalena were so simply proud and happy at having filled all their rooms for a month, that one could not help sharing their cheerfulness. Don A. was of a mechanical turn, and I heard that he also earned something by repairing the watches of peasants who could not or would not pay for finer surgery. Greater gentleness, sweeter kindliness never surrounded the inmates of hired lodgings than enveloped us in the manners of this good priest and his niece. They did together all the work of the apartment, serving us without shame and without reluctance, yet keeping a soft dignity withal that was extremely pretty. May no word of mine offend them, for every word of theirs was meant to make us feel at home with them; and I believe that they will not mind this public recognition of the grace with which they adorned their gentle poverty. They never intruded, but they were always there, saluting our outgoing and incoming, and watchful of our slightest wish. Often before we could get our key into the outer door Maddalena had run to open it, holding her *lucerna* above her head to light us, and hailing us with a *"Buona sera Loro!"* (Good-evening to them – our lordships, namely) to which only music could do justice.

But the landlord of the pension below, where we took our meals, was no less zealous for the comfort of his guests, and at that table of his, good at any price, and wonderful for the little they gave, he presided with a hospitality which pressed them to eat of this and that, and kept the unstinted wine a-flowing, and communicated itself to Luigi, who, having cooked the dinner, hurled on a dress-coat of impenetrable antiquity and rushed in to help serve it; and to Angiolina, the housekeeper, who affected a sort of Yankee old-maid's grumpiness, but was as sweet of soul as Maddalena herself. More than once has that sympathetic spirit, in passing me a dish, advised me with a fine movement of her clasping thumb which morsel to choose.

We took our rooms in the belief that we were on the sunny side of the house; and so we were; the sun obliquely bathed that whole front of the edifice, and I never can understand why it should not have got in-doors. It did not; but it was delightful in the garden which stretched from the rear of our palace across to the city wall. Just under our windows – but far under, for we were in the fourth story – was a wide stone terrace, old, moss-grown, balustraded with marble, from which you descended by two curving flights of marble steps into the garden. There, in the early March weather, which succeeded a wind-storm of three days, the sun fell like a shining silence, amidst which the bent figure of an old gardener stirred, noiselessly turning up the earth. In the utmost distance the snow-covered Apennines glistened against a milky white sky growing pale blue above; the nearer hills were purplish; nearer yet were green fields, gray olive orchards, red plowed land, and black cypress-clumps about the villas with which the whole prospect was thickly sown. Then the city houses outside the wall began, and then came the beautiful red brick city wall, wandering wide over the levels and heights and hollows, and within it that sunny silence of a garden. While I once stood at the open window looking, brimful of content, tingling with it, a bugler came up the road without the wall, and gayly, bravely sounded a gallant *fanfare*, purely, as it seemed, for love of it and pleasure in it.

I call our garden a garden, but it was mostly a succession of fields, planted with vegetables for the market, and closed round next the city wall with ranks of olive-trees. Still, next the palace there were flowers, or must have been in summer; and on another morning, another heavenly morning, a young lady, doubtless of the ancient family to which the palace belonged, came out upon the terrace from the first floor with an elderly companion, and, loitering listlessly there a moment, descended the steps into the garden to a stone basin where some serving-women were washing. Her hair was ashen blonde; she was slimly cased in black silk, and as she slowly walked, she pulled forward the skirt a little with one hand, while she drew together with the other a light shawl, falling from the top of her head, round her throat; her companion followed at a little distance; on the terrace lingered a large white Persian cat, looking after them.

## VIII.

These gardens, or fields, of Siena occupy half the space her walls enclose, and the olives everywhere softly embower the borders of the shrivelled and shrunken old city, which once must have plumply filled their circuit with life. But it is five hundred years since the great pest reduced her hundred thousand souls to fifteen thousand; generation after generation the plow has gone over the dead streets, and the spade has been busy obliterating the decay, so that now there is no sign of them where the artichokes stretch their sharp lines, and the tops of the olives run tangling in the wind. Except where the streets carry the lines of buildings to the ten gates,

the city is completely surrounded by these gardens within
its walls; they drop on all sides from the lofty ledge of rocks
to which the edifices cling, with the cathedral pre-eminent,
and cover the slopes with their herbage and foliage; at one
point near the Lizza, flanking the fort which Cosimo built
where the Spaniards failed, a gaunt ravine – deep, lonely,
shadowy – pushes itself up into the heart of the town. Once,
and once only, so old is the decay of Siena, I saw the crum-
bling foundations of a house on a garden slope; but again and
again the houses break away, and the street which you have
been following ceases in acreages of vegetation. Sometimes
the varied and ever-picturesquely irregular ground has the
effect of having fallen away from the palaces; the rear of a line
of these, at one point, rested on massive arches, with but-
tresses sprung fifty or seventy-five feet from the lower level;
and on the lofty shoulders of the palaces, here and there, was
caught a bit of garden, and lifted with its overhanging hedge
high into the sun. There are abundant evidences of that lost
beauty and magnificence of Siena – she has kept enough
of both – not only in the great thirteenth and fourteenth
century structures in the Via Cavour, the Via del Capitano,
and the neighborhood of the Palazzo Communale, but in
many little wandering, darkling streets, where you come
upon exquisite Gothic arches walled up in the fronts of now
ordinary houses, which before some time of great calamity
must have been the portals and windows of noble palaces.
These gave their pathos to walks which were bewilderingly
opulent in picturesqueness; walks that took us down sharp
declivities dropping under successive arches between the
house-walls, and flashing out upon sunny prospects of gardens; up steep thoroughfares climbing and crooking from the

gates below, and stopping as if for rest in successive piazzas, till they reach the great avenue which stretches along the high spine of the city from Porta Camollia to Porta Romana. Sharp turns everywhere bring your nose against some incomparable piece of architecture, or your eye upon some view astonishingly vast, and smiling or austere, but always enchanting.

The first night we found the Via Cavour full of people, walking and talking together; and there was always the effect of out-door liveliness in the ancient town, which is partly to be accounted for by the pungent strength of the good air. This stirs and sustains one like the Swiss air, and when not in too rapid motion it is delicious. In March I will own that its motion was often too rapid. It swept cold from the Apennines, and one night it sifted the gray depths of the streets full of snow. The next morning the sun blazed out with that ironical smile which we know here as well as in Italy, and Via Cavour was full of people lured forth by his sarcastic glitter, though the wind blew pitilessly. *"Marzo matto!"* (Crazy March!) said the shopman, with a sympathetic smile and impressive shrug, to whom I complained of it; and I had to confess that March was no better in America. The peasants, who took the whole breadth of Via Cavour with their carts laden with wine and drawn by wide-horned dun oxen, had their faces tied up against the blast, which must have been terrible on their hills; and it roared and blustered against our lofty eyry in Palazzo Bandini-Piccolomini with a force that penetrated it with icy cold. It was quite impossible to keep warm; with his back planted well into the fire-place blazing with the little logs of the country, and fenced about on the windward side with mattresses and sofa-pillows, a suffering novelist was able to complete his then current fiction only at the risk of freezing.

But before this, and after it, we had weather in which the streets were as much a pleasure to us as to the Sienese; and in fact I do not know where I would rather be at this moment than in Via Cavour, unless it were on the Grand Canal at Venice – or the Lungarno at Florence – or the Pincio at Rome – or Piazza Brà at Verona. Any of these places would do, and yet they would all lack the strictly mediæval charm which belongs to Siena, and which perhaps you feel most when you stand before the Tolomei Palace, with its gray Gothic façade, on the richly sculptured porch of the Casino dei Nobili. At more than one point the gaunt Roman wolf suckles her adoptive twins on the top of a pillar; and the olden charm of prehistoric fable mingles with the interest of the city's proper life, when her people fought each other for their freedom in her streets, and never trusted one another except in some fiery foray against the enemy beyond her gates.

Let the reader not figure to himself any broad, straight level when I speak of Via Cavour as the principal street; it is only not so narrow and steep and curving as the rest, and a little more light gets into it; but there is one level, and one alone, in all Siena, and that is the lizza, the public promenade, which looks very much like an artificial level. It is planted with pleasant little bosks and trim hedges, beyond which lurk certain cafés and beer-houses, and it has walks and a drive. On a Sunday afternoon of February, when the military band played there, and I was told that the fine world of Siena resorted to the Lizza, we hurried thither to see it; but we must have come too late. The band were blowing the drops of distilled music out of their instruments and shutting them up, and on the drive there was but one equipage worthy of the name. Within this carriage sat a little refined-looking boy, – delicate, pale, the expression of an effete aristocracy; and beside him sat a very stout, gray-mustached, side-whiskered, eagle-nosed, elderly gentleman, who took snuff out of a gold box, and looked like Old Descent in person. I felt, at sight of them, that I had met the Sienese nobility, whom otherwise I did not see; and yet I do not say that they may not have been a prosperous fabricant of panforte and his son. A few young bucks, with fierce trotting-ponies in two-seated sulkies, hammered round the drive; the crowd on foot was mostly a cloaked and slouch-hatted crowd, which in Italy is always a plebeian crowd. There were no ladies, but many women of less degree, pretty enough, well-dressed enough, and radiantly smiling. In the centre of the place shone a resplendent group of officers, who kept quite to themselves. We could not feel that we had mingled greatly in the social gayeties of Siena, and we wandered off to climb the bastions of the old Medicean fort – very bold with its shield and *palle* over the gateway – and listened to the bees humming in the oleander hedge beneath.

This was toward the end of February; a few days later I find it recorded that in walking half-way round the city outside the wall I felt the sun very hot, and heard the birds singing over the fields, where the peasants were breaking the clods with their hoes. The almond-trees kept blossoming with delicate courage all through February, like girls who brave the lingering cold with their spring finery; and though the grass was green, with here and there daring dandelions in it, the landscape generally had a pathetic look of winter weariness, when we drove out into the country beyond the wall.

It is this wall with the color of its red brick which everywhere warms up the cold gray tone of Siena. It is like no other city wall that I know, except that of Pisa, and is not supported with glacis on the inside, but rises sheer from the earth there as on the outside. With its towers and noble gates it is beautiful always; and near the railway station it obligingly abounds in repaired spots which look as if they had been holes knocked in it at the great siege. I hope they were.

It is anywhere a study for a painter – preferably a water-colorist, I should say – and I do not see how an architect could better use his eyes in Italy than in perusing the excellent brick-work of certain of the smaller houses, as well as certain palaces and churches, both in the city and the suburbs of Siena. Some of the carved brick there is delightful, and the material is treated with peculiar character and feeling.

## IX.

The ancient palace of the Republic, the Palazzo Communale, is of brick, which allegorizes well enough the multitude of plebeian wills and forces that went to the constitution of the democratic state. No friend of popular rule, I suppose, can boast that these little mediæval commonwealths of Italy were the homes of individual liberty. They were popular tyrannies; but tyrannies as they were, they were always better than the single-handed despotisms, the *governo d'un solo*, which supplanted them, except in the one fact only that they did not give continuous civil peace. The crater of the extinct volcano before the Palazzo Communale in Siena was always boiling with human passions, and for four hundred years it vomited up and ingulfed innumerable governments and forms of government, now aristocratic and now plebeian. From those beautiful Gothic windows many a traitor has dangled head downwards or feet downwards, as the humor took the mob; many a temporizer or usurper has hurtled from that high balcony ruining down to the stones below.

Carlo Folletti-Fossati, a Sienese citizen of our own time, has made a luminous and interesting study of the "Costumi Senese" of the Middle Ages, which no reader of Italian should fail to get when he goes to Siena, for the sake of the light which it throws upon that tumultuous and struggling past of one of the bravest and doughtiest little peoples that ever lived. In his chapters on the "Daily Life" of the Sienese of those times, he speaks first of the world-wide difference between the American democracy and the mediæval democracies. He has read his De Tocqueville, and he understands, as Mr. Matthew Arnold is beginning to understand, that the secret of our political success is in the easy and natural fit of our political government, the looseness of our social organization; and he shows with attractive clearness how, in the Italian republics, there was no conception of the popular initiative, except in the matter of revolution, which was extra-constitutional. The government once established, no matter how democratic, how plebeian its origin, it began at once to interfere with the personal affairs of the people. It regulated their household expenses; said what dishes and how many they might have at dinner; clipped women's gowns, and forbade the braid and laces on their sleeves and stomachers; prescribed the fashion of men's hats and cloaks; determined the length of coats, the size of bricks, and the dimensions of letter-paper; costumed the different classes; established the hours of pleasure and business; limited the number of those who should be of this or that trade or profession; bothered in every way. In Siena, at a characteristic period, the signory were chosen every two months, and no man might decline the honor and burden of office except under heavy fine. The government must have been as great a bore to its officers as to its subjects, for, once elected, the signory were obliged to remain night and day in the public palace. They could not leave it except for some grave reason of state, or sickness, or marriage, or the death of near kindred, and then they could only go out two at a time, with a third for a spy upon them. Once a week they could converse with the citizens, but solely on public business. Then, on Thursdays, the signory – the Nine, or the Twelve, or the Priors, whichever they chanced to be – descended from their magnificent confinement in the apartments of state to the great hall of the ground floor, and heard the petitions of all comers. Otherwise, their official life was no joke: in the months of March and April, 1364, they consumed in their public labors eleven reams of paper, twenty-one quires of parchment, twelve pounds of red and green sealing-wax, five hundred goose-quills, and twenty bottles of ink.

Besides this confinement at hard labor, they were obliged to suffer from the shrieks of the culprits, who were mutilated or put to death in the rear of the palace; for in those days prison expenses were saved by burning a witch or heretic, tearing out the tongue of a blasphemer, striking off the right hand of a perjurer or bigamist, and the right foot of a highwayman. The Sienese in course of time became so refined that they expelled the mutilated wretches from the city, that they might not offend the eye, after the infliction of their penalties; but in the mean while the signory could not bear the noise of their agony, especially while they sat at dinner; and the execution-grounds were finally changed to a remote quarter.

It is well enough for the tourist to give a thought to these facts and conditions of the times that produced the beautiful architecture of the Palazzo Communale and the wonderful frescos which illumine its dim-vaulted halls and chambers. The masters who wrought either might have mixed the mortar for their bricks, and the colors for their saints and angels, and allegories and warriors, with human blood, it flowed so freely and abundantly in Siena. Poor, splendid, stupid, glorious past! I stood at the windows of the people's palace and looked out on the space in the rear where those culprits used to disturb the signory at their meals, and thanked Heaven that I was of the nineteenth century. The place is flanked now by an immense modern prison, whose ample casements were crowded with captives pressing to them for the sun; and in the distance there is a beautiful view of an insane asylum, the largest and most populous in Italy.

I suppose the reader will not apprehend a great deal of comment from me upon the frescos, inexpressibly quaint and rich, from which certain faces and certain looks remain with me yet. The pictures figure the great scenes of Sienese history and fable. There are the battles in which the republic triumphed, to the disadvantage chiefly of the Florentines; there are the victorious encounters of her son

Pope Alexander III. with Barbarossa; there are allegories in
which her chief citizens appear. In one of these – I think it
is that representing "Good and Bad Government," painted
by Lorenzetti in 1337 – there is a procession of Sienese
figures and faces of the most curious realistic interest, and
above their heads some divine and august ideal shapes, – a
Wisdom, from whose strange eyes all mystery looks, and
a Peace and a Fortitude which, for an unearthly dignity
and beauty, I cannot remember the like of. There is also,
somewhere in those dusky halls, a most noble St. Victor
by Sodoma; and I would not have my readers miss that sly
rogue of a saint ("We are famous for our saints in Siena,"
said the sardonic custodian, with a shrug) who is represented
in a time of interdict stealing a blessing from the Pope for
his city by having concealed under his cloak a model of it
when he appears before the pontiff! For the rest, there is an
impression of cavernous gloom left from many of the rooms
of the palace which characterizes the whole to my memory;
and as I look back into it, beautiful, mystical, living eyes
glance out of it; noble presences, solemn attitudes, forms
of grandeur faintly appear; and then all is again a hovering
twilight, out of which I am glad to emerge into the laughing
sunshine of the piazza.

## X.

A monument of the old magnanimity of Siena is that Capella
di Piazza in front of the palace, at the foot of the tower,
which the tourist goes to see for the sake of Sodoma's fresco
in it, but which deserves to be also revered as the memorial
of the great pest of 1348; it was built in 1352, and thrice

demolished and thrice rebuilt before it met with public approval. This and the beautiful Fonte Gaja – as beautiful in its way as the tower – make the piazza a place to linger in and come back to at every chance. The fountain was designed by Giacomo della Quercia, who was known thereafter as Giacomo della Fonte, and it was called the Gay Fountain in memory of the festivities with which the people celebrated the introduction of good water into their city in 1419. Seven years the artist wrought upon it, and three thousand florins of gold the republic paid for the work, which after four hundred years has been restored in all its first loveliness by Tito Sarocchi, an admirable Sienese sculptor of our day.

There are six fountains in all, in different quarters of the city; and of these, the finest are the two oldest, – Fonte Branda of the twelfth century, and Fonte Nuova of the fourteenth. Fonte Branda I will allow to be the more famous, but never so beautiful as Fonte Nuova. They are both as practicable now as when they were built, and Fonte Nuova has a small house atop of its arches, where people seem to live. The arches are Gothic, and the delicate carved brick-work of Siena decorates their sharp spring. Below, in the bottom of the four-sided structure, is the clear pool from whose affluent pipes the neighborhood comes to draw its water (in buckets hammered from solid copper into antique form), and in which women seem to be always rinsing linen, or beating it with wooden paddles in the Latin fashion.

Fonte Branda derives a world-wide celebrity from being mentioned by Dante and then having its honors disputed by a small stream of its name elsewhere. It, too, is a lovely Gothic shape, and whenever I saw it wash-day was in possession of it. The large pool which the laundresses had whitened with their suds is used as a swimming-vat in summer; and the old fountain may therefore be considered in very active use still, so many years after Dante dedicated the new fountain to disputed immortality with a single word. It was one of those extremely well-ventilated days of March when I last visited Fonte Branda; and not only was the linen of all Siena blowing about from balconies and house-tops, but, from a multitude of galleries and casements, hides of leather were lustily flapping and giving out the pungent aroma of the tan. It is a region of tanneries, and some of them are of almost as august a presence as the Fonte Branda itself. We had not come to see either, but to pay our second visit to the little house of St. Catherine of Siena, who was born and lived a child in this neighborhood, the good Contrada dell' Oca, or Goose Ward, which took this simple name while other wards of Siena called themselves after the Dragon, the Lion, the Eagle, and other noble beasts and birds. The region has therefore the odor of sanctity as well as of leather, and is consecrated by the memory of one of the best and bravest and meekest woman's lives ever lived. Her house here is much visited by the curious and devout, and across a chasmed and gardened space from the fountain rises high on the bluff the high-shouldered bulk of the church of San Domenico, in which Catherine was first rapt in her beatific visions of our Lord, conversing with him, and giving him her heart for his in mystical espousals.

## XI.

EW strangers in Siena fail to visit the house where that great woman and saint, Caterina Benincasa, was born in 1347. She was one of a family of thirteen or fourteen children, that blessed the union of Giacomo and Lapa, who were indeed well-in-the-house as their name is, being interpreted; for with the father's industry as a dyer, and the mother's thrift, they lived not merely in decent poverty, but in sufficient ease; and it was not from a need of her work nor from any want of piety in themselves that her parents at first opposed her religious inclination, but because (as I learn from the life of her written by that holy man, G. B. Francesia), hearing on every side the praises of her beauty and character, they hoped to make a splendid marriage for her. When she persisted in her prayers and devotions, they scolded and beat her, as good parents used to do, and made her the household drudge. But one day while the child was at prayer the father saw a white dove hovering over her head, and though she said she knew nothing of it, he was struck with awe and ceased to persecute her. She was now fourteen, and at this time she began her penances, sleeping little on the hard floor where she lay, scourging herself continually, wearing a hair shirt, and lacerating her flesh with chains. She fell sick, and was restored to health only by being allowed to join a sisterhood, under the rule of St. Dominic, who were then doing many good works in Siena. After that our Lord began to appear to her in the Dominican church; she was likewise tempted of the devil; but Christ ended by making her his spouse. While her ecstasies continued she not only visited the sick and poor, but she already took an interest in public affairs, appealing first to the rival factions in Siena to mitigate their furies, and then trying to make peace between the Ghibellines of that city and the Guelphs of Florence. She pacified many family feuds; multitudes thronged to see her and hear her; and the

Pope authorized her to preach throughout the territory of Siena. While she was thus dedicated to the salvation of souls, war broke out afresh between the Sienese and Florentines, and in the midst of it the terrible pest appeared. Then the saint gave herself up to the care of the sick, and performed miracles of cure, at the same time suffering persecution from the suspicions of the Sienese, among whom question of her patriotism arose.

She now began also to preach a new crusade against the Saracens, and for this purpose appeared in Pisa. She went later to Avignon to beseech the Pope to remove an interdict laid upon the Florentines, and then she prevailed with him to remove his court to the ancient seat of St. Peter.

The rest of her days were spent in special miracles; in rescuing cities from the plague; in making peace between the different Italian states and between all of them and the Pope; in difficult journeys; in preaching and writing. "And two years before she died," says her biographer, "the truth manifested itself so clearly in her, that she prayed certain scriveners to put in writing what she should say during her ecstasies. In this manner there was soon composed the treatise on Obedience and Prayer, and on Divine Providence, which contains a dialogue between a Soul and God. She dictated as rapidly as if reading, in a clear voice, with her eyes closed and her arms crossed on her breast and her hands opened her limbs became so rigid that, having ceased to speak, she remained a long hour silent; then, holy water being sprinkled in her face, she revived." She died in Rome in 1380; but even after her death she continued to work miracles; and her head was brought amidst great public rejoicings to her native city. A procession went out to receive it, led by the Senate, the Bishop of Siena, and all the bishops of the state, with all the secular and religious orders. "That which was wonderful and memorable on this occasion," says the Diario Senese, "was that Madonna Lapa, mother of our Seraphic Compatriot, – who had many years before restored her to life, and liberated her from the pains of hell, – was led to the solemn encounter."

It seems by all accounts to have been one of the best and strongest heads that ever rested on a woman's shoulders – or a man's, for the matter of that; apt not only for private beneficence, but for high humane thoughts and works of great material and universal moment; and I was willing to see the silken purse, or sack, in which it was brought from Rome, and which is now to be viewed in the little chamber where she used to pillow the poor head so hard. I do not know that I wished to come any nearer the saint's mortal part, but our Roman Catholic brethren have another taste in such matters, and the body of St. Catherine has been pretty well dispersed about the world to supply them with objects of veneration. One of her fingers, as I learn from the Diario Senese of Girolamo Gigli (the most confusing, not to say stupefying, form of history I ever read, being the collection under the three hundred and sixty-five several days of the year of all the events happening on each in Siena since the time of Remus's son), is in the Certosa at Pontignano, where it has been seen by many, to their great advantage, with the wedding-ring of Jesus Christ upon it. Her right thumb is in the church of the Dominicans at Camporeggi; one of her ribs is in the cathedral at Siena; another in the church of the Company of St. Catherine, from which a morsel has been sent to the same society in the city of Lima,

in Peru; her cervical vertebra and one of her slippers are
treasured by the Nuns of Paradise; in the monastery of Sts.
Dominic and Sixtus at Rome is her right hand; her shoulder
is in the convent of St. Catherine at Magnanopoli; and her
right foot is in the church of San Giovanni e Paolo at Venice.
In St. Catherine at Naples are a shoulder-bone and a finger;
in other churches there are a piece of an arm and a rib; in San
Bartolomeo at Salerno there is a finger; the Predicatori at
Colonia have a rib; the Canons of Eau-Court in Artois have
a good-sized bone (*osso di giusta grandezza*); and the good
Gigli does not know exactly what bone it is they revere in
the Chapel Royal at Madrid. But perhaps this is enough, as
it is.

## XII.

The arched and pillared front of St. Catherine's house is
turned toward a street on the level of Fonte Branda, but
we reached it from the level above, whence we clambered
down to it by a declivity that no carriage could descend.
It has been converted, up stairs and down, into a number
of chapels, and I suppose that the ornate façade dates from
the ecclesiastic rather than the domestic occupation. Of a
human home there are indeed few signs, or none, in the
house; even the shop in which the old dyer, her father,
worked at his trade has been turned into a chapel and enriched, like the rest, with gold and silver, gems and precious
marbles.

From the house we went to the church of San Domenico,
hard by, and followed St. Catherine's history there through
the period of her first ecstasies, in which she received the

stigmata and gave her heart to her heavenly Spouse in exchange for his own. I do not know how it is with other Protestants, but for myself I will confess that in the place where so many good souls for so many ages have stood in the devout faith that the miracles recorded really happened there, I could not feel otherwise than reverent. Illusion, hallucination as it all was, it was the error of one of the purest souls that ever lived, and of one of the noblest minds. "Here," says the printed tablet appended to the wall of the chapel, "here she was invested with the habit of St. Dominic; and she was the first woman who up to that time had worn it. Here she remained withdrawn from the world, listening to the divine services of the church, and here continually in divine colloquy she conversed familiarly with Jesus Christ, her Spouse. Here, leaning against this pilaster, she was rapt in frequent ecstasies; wherefore this pilaster has ever since been potent against the infernal furies, delivering many possessed of devils." Here Jesus Christ appeared before her in the figure of a beggar, and she gave him alms, and he promised to own her before all the world at the Judgment Day. She gave him her robe, and he gave her an invisible garment which forever after kept her from the cold. Here once he gave her the Host himself, and her confessor, missing it, was in great terror till she told him. Here the Lord took his own heart from his breast and put it into hers.

You may also see in this chapel, framed and covered with a grating in the floor, a piece of the original pavement on which Christ stood and walked. The whole church is full of memories of her; and there is another chapel in it, painted in fresco by Sodoma with her deeds and miracles, which in its kind is almost incomparably rich and beautiful.

It is the painter's most admirable and admired work, in which his genius ranges from the wretch decapitated in the bottom of the picture to the soul borne instantly aloft by two angels in response to St. Catherine's prayers. They had as much nerve as faith in those days, and the painter has studied the horror with the same conscience as the glory. It would be interesting to know how much he believed of what he was painting, – just as it would be now to know how much I believe of what I am writing: probably neither of us could say.

What impresses St. Catherine so vividly upon the fancy that has once begun to concern itself with her is the double character of her greatness. She was not merely an ecstatic nun: she was a woman of extraordinary political sagacity, and so great a power among statesmen and princes that she alone could put an end to the long exile of the popes at Avignon, and bring them back to Rome. She failed to pacify her country because, as the Sienese historian Buonsignore confesses, "the germs of the evil were planted so deeply that it was beyond human power to uproot them." But, nevertheless, "she rendered herself forever famous by her civic virtues," her active beneficence, her perpetual striving for the good of others, all and singly; and even so furious a free-thinker as the author of my "New Guide to Siena" thinks that, setting aside the marvels of legend, she has a right to the reverence of posterity, the veneration of her fellow-citizens. "St. Catherine, an honor to humanity, is also a literary celebrity: the golden purity of her diction, the sympathetic and affectionate simplicity of expression in her letters, still arouse the admiration of the most illustrious writers. With the potency of her prodigious genius, the virgin stainlessness of her life, and her great heart warm with love of country and magnanimous desires, inspired by a sublime ideal even in her mysticism, she, born of the people, meek child of Giacomo the dyer, lifted herself to the summit of religious and political grandeur. . . . With an overflowing eloquence and generous indignation she stigmatized the crimes, the vices, the ambition of the popes, their temporal power, and the scandalous schism of the Roman Church."

In the Communal Library at Siena I had the pleasure of seeing many of St. Catherine's letters in the MS. in which they were dictated: she was not a scholar like the great Socinus, whose letters I also saw, and she could not even write.

### XIII.

A hundred years after St. Catherine's death there was born in the same "noble Ward of the Goose" one of the most famous and eloquent of Italian reformers, the Bernardino Ochino, whose name commemorates that of his native Contrada dell' Oca. He became a Franciscan, and through the austerity of his life, the beauty of his character, and the wonder of his eloquence he became the General of his Order in Italy, and then he became a Protestant. "His words could move stones to tears," said Charles V., and when he preached in Siena, no space was large enough for his audience except the great piazza before the Public Palace, which was thronged even to the house-tops. Ochino escaped by flight the death that overtook his sometime fellow-denizen of Siena, Aonio Paleario, whose book, "Il Beneficio di Cristo," was very famous in its time and potent for reform throughout Italy.

In that doughty little Siena, in fact, there has been almost as much hard thinking as hard fighting, and what with Ochino and Paleario, with Socinus and Bandini, the Reformation, Rationalism, and Free Trade may be said almost to have been invented in the city which gave one of the loveliest and sublimest saints to the Church. Let us not forget, either, that brave archbishop of Siena, Ascanio Piccolomini, one of the ancient family which gave two popes to Rome, and which in this archbishop had the heart to defy the Inquisition and welcome Galileo to the protection of an inviolable roof.

## XIV.

It is so little way off from Fonte Branda and St. Catherine's house, that I do not know but the great cathedral of Siena may also be in the "Ward of the Goose;" but I confess that I did not think of this when I stood before that wondrous work.

There are a few things in this world about whose grandeur one may keep silent with dignity and advantage, as St. Mark's, for instance, and Nôtre Dame, and Giotto's Tower, and the curve of the Arno at Pisa, and Niagara, and the cathedral at Siena. I am not sure that one has not here more authority for holding his peace than before any of the others. Let the architecture go, then: the inexhaustible treasure of the sculptured marbles, the ecstasy of Gothic invention, the splendor of the mosaics, the quaintness, the grotesqueness, the magnificence of the design and the detail. The photographs do well enough in suggestion for such as have not seen the church, but these will never have the full sense of it which only long looking and coming again and again can impart. One or two facts, however, may be imagined, and the reader may fancy the cathedral set on the crest of the noble height to which Siena clings, and from which the streets and houses drop all round from the narrow level expressed in the magnificent stretch of that straight line with which the cathedral-roof delights the eye from every distance. It has a preeminence which seems to me unapproached, and this structure, which only partially realizes the vast design of its founders, impresses one with the courage even more than the piety of the little republic, now so utterly extinct. What a force was in men's hearts in those days! What a love of beauty must have exalted the whole community!

The Sienese were at the height of their work on the great cathedral when the great pestilence smote them, and broke them forever, leaving them a feeble phantom of their past glory and prosperity. "The infection," says Buonsignore, "spread not only from the sick, but from everything they touched; and the terror was such that selfish frenzy mounted to the wildest excess; not only did neighbor abandon neighbor, friend forsake friend, but the wife her husband, parents their children. In the general fear, all noble and endearing feelings were hushed. . . . Such was the helplessness into which the inhabitants lapsed that the stench exhaling from the wretched huts of the poor was the sole signal of death within. The dead were buried by a few generous persons whom an angelic pity moved to the duty: their appeal was, 'Help to carry this body to the grave, that when we die others may bear us thither!' The proportion of the dead to the sick was frightful; out of every five seized by the plague, scarcely one survived. Angelo di Tura tells us that at Siena, in the months of May, June, July, and August of the year 1348, the pest carried off eighty thousand persons. . . . A hundred noble familes were extinguished." Throughout Italy, "three fourths of the population perished. The cities, lately flourishing, busy, industrious, full of life, had become squalid, deserted, bereft of the activity which promotes grandeur. In Siena the region of Fonte Branda was largely saved from the infection by the odor of its tanneries. Other quarters, empty and forsaken, were set on fire after the plague ceased, and the waste areas where they stood became the fields and gardens we now see within the walls. . . . The work on the cathedral, which had gone forward for ten years, was suspended, . . . and when resumed, it was upon a scale adjusted to the diminished wealth of the city, and the plan was restricted to the dimensions which we now behold. . . . And if the fancy contemplates the grandeur of the original project, divining it from the vestiges of the walls and the columns remaining imperfect, but still preserved in good condition, it must be owned that the republic disposed of resources of which we can form no conception; and we must rest astounded that a little state, embroiled in perpetual wars with its neighbors, and in the midst of incessant party strife, should undertake the completion of a work worthy of the greatest and most powerful nations."

"When a man," says Mr. Addison, writing from Siena in the spirit of the genteel age which he was an ornament of, "sees the prodigious pains and expense that our forefathers have been at in these barbarous buildings, one cannot but fancy to himself what miracles of architecture they would have left us had they only been instructed in the right way; for when the devotion of those ages was much warmer than it is at present, and the riches of the people much more at the disposal of the priests, there was so much money consumed on these Gothic cathedrals as would have finished a greater variety of noble buildings than have been raised either before or since that time." And describing this wonderful cathedral of Siena in detail, he says that "nothing in the world can make a prettier show to those who prefer false beauties and affected ornaments to a noble and majestic simplicity."

The time will no doubt come again when we shall prefer "noble and majestic simplicity," as Mr. Addison did; and I for one shall not make myself the mock of it by confessing how much better I now like "false beauties and affected ornaments." In fact, I am willing to make a little interest with it by admitting that the Tuscan fashion of alternate courses of black and white marble in architecture robs the interior of the cathedral of all repose, and that nowhere else does the godless joke which nicknamed a New York temple "the Church of the Holy Zebra" insist upon itself so much. But if my business were iconoclasm, I should much rather smash the rococo apostolic statues which Mr. Addison doubtless admired, perching on their brackets at the base of the variegated pillars; and I suspect they are greatly to blame for the distraction which the visitor feels before he loses himself in the inexhaustibly beautiful and delightful detail. Shall I attempt to describe this? Not I! Get photographs, get prints, dear reader, or go see for yourself! Otherwise, trust me that if we had a tithe of that lavish loveliness in one structure in America, the richness of that one would impoverish the effect of all the other buildings on the continent. I say this, not with the hope of imparting an idea of the beauty, which words cannot, but to give some notion of the wealth poured out upon this mere fragment of what was meant to be the cathedral of Siena, and to help the reader conceive not only of the piety of the age, but of the love of art then universally spread among the Italians.

The day was abominably cold, of course, – it had been snowing that morning, – when we first visited the church, and I was lurking about with my skull-cap on, my teeth chattering, and my hands benumbing in my pockets, when the little *valet de place* who had helped us not find a lodging espied us and leaped joyously upon us, and ran us hither and thither so proudly and loudly that one of the priests had to come and snub him back to quiet and decorum. I do not know whether this was really in the interest of decency, or of the succession of sacristans who, when the *valet* had been retired to the front door, took possession of us, and lifted the planking which preserves the famous engraved pavement, and showed us the wonderful pulpit and the rich chapels, and finally the library all frescoed by Pinturicchio with scenes from the lives of the two Sienese Piccolomini who were Popes Pius II and III.

This multiplicity of sacristans suffered us to omit nothing, and one of them hastened to point out the two flag-poles fastened to the two pillars nearest the high altar, which are said to be those of the great War Car of the Florentines, captured by the Sienese at Montaperto in 1260. "How," says my "New Guide," "how on earth, the stranger will ask, do we find here in the house of God, who shed his blood for all mankind, here in the temple consecrated to Mary, mother of every sweet affection, these two records of a terrible carnage between brothers, sons of the same country? Does it not seem as if these relics from the field of battle stand here to render Divinity accomplice of the rage and hate and vengeance of men? We know not how to answer this question; we must even add that the crucifix not far from the poles, in the chapel on the left of the transept, was borne by the Sienese, trusting for victory in the favor of God, upon the field of Montaperto."

I make haste to say that I was not a stranger disposed to perplex my "New Guide" with any such question, and that nothing I saw in the cathedral gave me so much satisfaction as these flag-poles. Ghibelline and Sienese as I had become as soon as I turned my back on Guelphic Florence, I exulted in these trophies of Montaperto with a joy which nothing matched except the pleasure I had in viewing the fur-lined canopy of the War Car, which is preserved in the Opera del Duomo, and from which the custodian bestowed upon my devotion certain small tufts of the fur. I have no question but this canopy and the flag-poles are equally genuine, and I counsel the reader by all means to see them.

There are many other objects to be seen in the curious museum of antique and mediæval art called the Opera del Duomo, especially the original sculptures of the Fonte Gaia; but the place is chiefly interesting as the outline, the colossal sketch in sculptured marble, of the cathedral as it was projected. The present structure rises amid the halting fragments of the mediæval edifice, which it has included in itself, without exceeding their extent; and from the roof there is an ineffable prospect of the city and the country, from which one turns again in still greater wonder to the church itself.

I had an even deeper sense of its vastness, – the least marvellous of its facts, – and a renewed sense of the

domestication of the Italian churches, when I went one
morning to hear a Florentine monk, famed for his eloquence, preach in the cathedral. An oblong canopy of coarse
gray canvas had been stretched overhead in part of the great
nave, to keep his voice from losing itself in the space around
and above. The monk, from a pulpit built against one of the
pillars, faced a dais, across the nave, where the archbishop
sat in his chair to listen, and the planked floor between
them was thronged with people sitting and standing, who
came and went, as if at home, with a continued clapping of
feet and banging of doors. All the time service was going
on at several side-altars, where squads of worshippers were
kneeling, indifferent alike to one another and to the sermon
of the monk. Some of his listeners, however, wore a look of
intense interest, and I myself was not without concern in his
discourse, for I perceived that it was all in honor and compassion of the captive of the Vatican, and full of innuendo
for the national government. It gave me some notion of
the difficulties with which that government has to contend,
and impressed me anew with its admirable patience and
forbearance. Italy is unified, but many interests, prejudices,
and ambitions are still at war within her unity.


## XV.

One night we of the Pension T. made a sentimental pil-
grimage to the cathedral, to see it by moonlight. The moon
was not so prompt as we, and at first we only had it on the
baptistery and the campanile, — a campanile to make one
almost forget the Tower of Giotto. But before we came
away one corner of the façade had caught the light, and

hung richly bathed, tenderly etherealized in it. What was gold, what was marble before, seemed transmuted to the luminous substance of the moonlight itself, and rested there like some translucent cloud that "stooped from heaven and took the shape" of clustered arch and final.

On the way home we passed the open portal of a palace, and made ourselves the guests of its noble court, now poured full of the moon, and dimly lighted by an exquisite lantern of beaten iron, which hung near a massive pillar at the foot of the staircase. The pillar divided the staircase, and lost its branchy top in the vault overhead; and there was something so consciously noble and dignified in the whole architectural presence that I should have been surprised to find that we had not stumbled upon an historic edifice. It proved to be the ancient palace of the Captain of the People, – and I will thank the reader to imagine me a finer name than Capitano del Popolo for the head of such a democracy as Siena, whose earliest government, according to Alessandro Sozzini, was popular, after the Swiss fashion. Now the palace is the residence and property of the Grattanelli family, who have restored it and preserved it in the mediæval spirit, so that I suppose it is, upon the whole, the best realization of a phase of the past which one can see. The present Count Grattanelli – who may be rather a marquis or a prince, but who is certainly a gentleman of enlightened taste, and of a due sense of his Siena – keeps an apartment of the palace open to the public, with certain of the rooms in the original state, and store of armor and weapons in which the consequence of the old Captains of the People fitly masquerades. One must notice the beautiful doors of inlaid wood in this apartment, which are of the count's or marquis's or prince's own design;

and not fail of two or three ceilings frescoed in dark colors, in dense, close designs and small panels, after what seems a fashion peculiar to Siena.

Now that I am in Boston, where there are so few private palaces open to the public, I wonder that I did not visit more of them in Siena; but I find no record of any such visits but this one in my note-books. It was not for want of inscriptional provocation to penetrate interiors that I failed to do so. They are tableted in Siena beyond almost anything I have seen. The villa outside the gate where the poet Manzoni once visited his daughter records the fact for the passing stranger; on the way to the station a house boasts that within it the dramatist Pietro Cossa, being there "the guest of his adored mother," wrote his Cecilia and the second act of his Sylla; in a palace near that of Socinus you are notified that Alfieri wrote several of his tragedies; and another proclaims that he frequented it "holding dear the friendship" of the lady of the house! In spite of all this, I can remember only having got so far as the vestibule and staircase – lovely and grand they were, too – of one of those noble Gothic palaces in Via Cavour; I was deterred from going farther by learning it was not the day when uninvited guests were received. I always kept in mind, moreover, the Palazzo Tolomei for the sake of that dear and fair lady who besought the traveller through purgatory

> "Ricorditi di me, che eon la Pia;
> Siena mi fè, diefecemi Maremma,"

and who was of the ancient name still surviving in Siena. Some say that her husband carried her to die of malaria in the marshes of the Maremma; some, that he killed her with his dagger; others, that he made his servants throw her from the window of his castle; and none are certain whether or no he had reason to murder her, – they used to think there could be a reason for murdering wives in his day; even the good Gigli, of the Diario Senese, speaks of that "giusto motivo" Messer Nello may possibly have had. What is certain is that Pia was the most beautiful woman in Italy; and what is still more certain is that she was not a Tolomei at all, but only the widow of a Tolomei. Perhaps it was prescience of this fact that kept me from visiting the Tolomei palace for her sake. At any rate, I did not visit it, though I often stopped in the street before it, and dedicated a mistaken sigh to the poor lady who was only a Tolomei by marriage.

There were several other ladies of Siena, in past ages, who interested me. Such an one was the exemplary Onorata de' Principi Orsini, one of the four hundred Sienese noblewomen who went out to meet the Emperor Frederick III in 1341, when he came to Siena to espouse Leonora, Infanta of Portugal; a column near Porta Camollia still commemorates the exact spot where the Infanta stood to receive him. On this occasion the fair Onorata was, to the thinking of some of the other ladies, too simply dressed; but she defended herself against their censure, affirming that the "Sienese gentlewomen should make a pomp of nothing but their modesty, since in other displays and feminine adornments the matrons of other and richer cities could easily surpass them." And at a ball that night, being asked who was the handsomest gentleman present, she answered that she saw no one but her husband there. Is the estimable Onorata a trifle too sage for the reader's sympathy? Let him turn then to the Lady Battista Berti, wife of Achille Petrucci, who, at

another ball in honor of the Emperor, spoke Latin with him
so elegantly and with such spirit that he embraced her, and
created her countess, and begged her to ask some grace of
him; upon which this learned creature, instead of requesting
the Emperor to found a free public library, besought him to
have her exempted from the existing law which prohibited
the wearing of jewels and brocade dresses in Siena. The
careful Gigli would have us think that by this reply Lady
Battista lost all the credit which her Latinity had won her;
but it appears to me that both of these ladies knew very well
what they were about, and each in her way perceived that
the Emperor could appreciate a delicate stroke of humor
as well as another. If there were time, and not so many
questions of our own day pressing, I should like to inquire
into all the imaginable facts of these cases; and I commend
them to the reader, whose fancy cannot be so hard-worked
as mine.

The great siege of Siena by the Florentines and Imperial-
ists in 1554–55 called forth high civic virtues in the Sienese
women, who not only shared all the hardships and priva-
tions of the men, but often their labors, their dangers, and
their battles. "Never, Sienese ladies," gallantly exclaimed
the brave Blaise de Montluc, Marshal of France, who commanded the forces of the Most Christian King in defence of
the city, and who treats of the siege in his Commentaries,
"never shall I fail to immortalize your name so long as the
book of Montluc shall live; for in truth you are worthy of
immortal praise, if ever women were so. As soon as the
people took the noble resolution of defending their liberty,
the ladies of the city of Siena divided themselves into three
companies: the first was led by Lady Forteguerra, who was

dressed in violet, and all those who followed her likewise, having her accoutrement in the fashion of a nymph, short, and showing the buskin; the second by Lady Piccolomini, dressed in rose-colored satin, and her troops in the same livery; the third by Lady Livia Fausta, dressed in white, as was also all her following, and bearing a white ensign. On their flags they had some pretty devices; I would give a good deal if I could remember them. These three squadrons were composed of three thousand ladies, – gentlewomen or citizenesses. Their arms were pickaxes, shovels, baskets, and fascines; and thus equipped, they mustered and set to work on the fortifications. Monsieur de Termes, who has frequently told me about it (for I had not then arrived), has assured me that he never saw in his life anything so pretty as that. I saw the flags afterwards. They had made a song in honor of France, and they sang it in going to the fortifications. I would give the best horse I have if I could have been there. And since I am upon the honor of these ladies, I wish those who come after us to admire the courage of a young Sienese girl, who, although she was of poor condition, still deserves to be placed in the first rank. I had issued an order when I was chosen Dictator that nobody, on pain of being punished, should fail to go on guard in his turn. This girl, seeing her brother, whose turn it was, unable to go, takes his morion, which she puts on her head, his shoes, his buffalo-gorget; and with his halberd on her shoulders, goes off with the *corps de garde* in this guise, passing, when the roll is called, under the name of her brother, and stands sentinel in his place, without being known till morning. She was brought home in triumph. That afternoon Signor Cornelio showed her to me."

I am sorry that concerning the present ladies of Siena I know nothing except by the scantiest hearsay. My chief knowledge of them, indeed, centres in the story of one of the Borghesi there, who hold themselves so very much higher than the Borghesi of Rome. She stopped fanning herself a moment while some one spoke of them. "Oh, yes; I have heard that a branch of our family went to Rome. But I know nothing about them."

What glimpse we caught of Sienese society was at the theatre, – the lovely little theatre of the Accademia dei Rozzi. This is one of the famous literary academies of Italy; it was founded in the time of Leo X, and was then composed entirely of workingmen, who confessed their unpolished origin in their title; afterwards the Academies of the Wrapped-up, the Twisted, and the Insipid (such was the fantastic humor of the prevailing nomenclature) united with these Rude Men, and their academy finally became the most polite in Siena. Their theatre still enjoys a national fame, none but the best companies being admitted to its stage. We saw there the Rossi company of Turin, – the best players by all odds, after the great Florentine Stenterello, whom I saw in Italy. Commendatore Rossi's is an exquisite comic talent, – the most delicately amusing, the most subtly refined. In a comedy of Goldoni's ("A Curious Accident") which he gave, he was able to set the house in an uproar by simply letting a series of feelings pass over his face, in expression of the conceited, wilful old comedy-father's progress from facetious satisfaction in the elopement of his neighbor's daughter to a realization of the fact that it was his own daughter who had run away. Rossi, who must not be confounded with the tragedian of his name, is the first comedian who has ever been knighted in Italy, the theory being that since a comic actor might receive a blow which the exigency of the play forbade him to resent, he was unfit for knighthood. King Humbert seems somehow to have got over this prodigious obstacle.

The theatre was always filled, and between the acts there was much drama in the boxes, where the gentlemen went and came, making their compliments to the ladies, in the old Italian fashion. It looked very easy and pleasant; and I wish Count Nerli, whose box we had hired one evening when he sent the key to the ticket-office to be let, had been there to tell us something of the people in the others. I wish, in fact, that we might have known something of the count himself, whom, as it is, I know only by the title boldly lettered on his box-door. The acquaintance was slight, but very agreeable. Before the evening was out I had imagined him in a dozen figures and characters; and I still feel that I came very near knowing a Sienese count. Some English people, who became English friends, in our pension, had letters which took them into society, and they reported it very charming. Indeed, I heard at Florence, from others who knew it well, that it was pleasantly characterized by the number of cultivated people connected with the ancient university of Siena. Again, I heard that here, and elsewhere in Italy, husbands neglect their wives, and leave them dismal at home, while they go out to spend their evenings at the clubs and cafés. Who knows? I will not even pretend to do so, though the temptation is great.

A curious phase of the social life in another direction appeared in the notice which I found posted one day on the door of the church of San Cristoforo, inviting the poor girls of the parish to a competitive examination for the wedding-portions to be supplied to the most deserving from an ancient fund. They were advised that they must appear on some Sunday during Lent before the parish priest, with a petition certifying to these facts:

> "I. Poverty.
> "II. Good morals.
> "III. Regular attendance at church.
> "IV. Residence of six months in the parish.
> "V. Age between 18 and 30 years.
> "N.B. A girl who has won a dower in this or any other parish cannot compete."

## XVI.

The churches are very rich in paintings of the Sienese school, and the gallery of the Belle Arti, though small, is extremely interesting. Upon the whole, I do not know where one could better study the progress of Italian painting, from the Byzantine period up to the great moment when Sodoma came in Siena. Oddly enough, there was a very lovely little Bellini in this collection, which, with a small Veronese, distinguished itself from the Tuscan canvases, by the mellow beauty of the Venetian coloring, at once. It is worse than useless to be specific about pictures, and if I have kept any general impression of the Sienese work, it concerns the superior charm of the earlier frescos, especially in the Public Palace. In the churches the best frescos are at San Domenico, where one sees the exquisite chapel of St. Catherine painted by Sodoma, which I have already mentioned. After these one must reckon in interest the histories with which Pinturicchio has covered the whole library of the cathedral, and which are surpassingly delightful in their quaint realism. For the rest, I have a vivid memory of a tendency in the Sienese painters to the more horrific facts of Scripture and legend; they were terrible fellows for the Massacre of the Innocents, and treated it with a bloodier carefulness of detail than I remember to have noticed in any other school; the most sanguinary of these slaughters is in the Church of the Servi. But there is something wholesome and human even in the most butcherly of their simple-minded carnages; it is where the allegorists get hold of horror that it becomes loathsome, as in that choir of a church, which I have forgotten the name of, where the stalls are decorated with winged death's heads, the pinions shown dropping with rottenness and decay around the skulls. Yet this too had its effectiveness: it said what some people of that time were thinking; and I suppose that the bust of a lady in a fashionable ruff, with a book in her hand, simpering at the bust of her husband in an opposite niche in San Vigilio, was once not so amusing as it now looks. I am rather proud of discovering her, for I found her after I had been distinctly discouraged from exploring the church by the old woman in charge. She was civil, but went back eagerly to her gossip with another crone there, after saying: "The pictures in the roof are of no merit. They are beautiful, however." I liked this church, which was near our pension, because it seemed such a purely little neighborhood affair; and I must have been about the only tourist who ever looked into it.

One afternoon we drove out to the famous convent of the Osservanza, which was suppressed with the other convents, but in which the piety of charitable people still maintains

fifty of the monks. We passed a company of them, young
and old, on our way, bareheaded and barefooted, as their
use is, and looking very fit in the landscape; they saluted us
politely, and overtaking us in the porch of the church, rang
up the sacristan for us, and then, dropping for a moment
on one knee before the door, disappeared into the convent.
The chapel is not very much to see, though there is a most
beautiful Della Robbia there, – a Madonna and St. Thomas, –
which I would give much to see now. When we had gone the
round of the different objects, our sacristan, who was very
old and infirm, and visibly foul in the brown robes which
are charitable to so much dirt, rose from the last altar before
which he had knelt with a rheumatic's groans, and turning
to the ladies with a malicious grin, told them that they could
not be admitted to the cloisters, though the gentlemen could
come. We followed him through the long, dreary galleries,
yawning with hundreds of empty cells, and a sense of the
obsoleteness of the whole affair oppressed me. I do not
know why this feeling should have been heightened by the
smallness of the gardened court enclosed by the cloisters,
or by the tinkle of a faint old piano coming from some room
where one of the brothers was practising. The whole place
was very bare, and stared with fresh whitewash; but from
the pervading smell I feared that this venerable relic of the
past was not well drained, – though I do not know that in
the religious ages they valued plumbing greatly, anywhere.


## XVII.

In this and other drives about Siena the peculiar character of the volcanic landscape made itself continually felt.

There is a desolation in the treeless hills, and a wildnses and strangeness in their forms, which I can perhaps beet suggest by repeating that they have been constantly reproduced by the Tuscan painters in their backgrounds, and that most Judean landscapes in their pictures are faithful studies of such naked and lonely hills as billow round Siena. The soil is red, and but for the wine and oil with which it flows, however reluctantly, I should say that it must be poor. Some of the hills look mere heaps of clay, such as mighty geysers might have cast up until at last they hid themselves under the accumulation; and this seems to be the nature of the group amidst which the battle of Montaperto was fought. I speak from a very remote inspection, for though we started to drive there, we considered, after a mile or two, that we had no real interest in it now, either as Florentines or Sienese, and contented ourselves with a look at the Arbia, which the battle "colored red," but which had long since got back its natural complexion. This stream – or some other which the driver passed off on us for it – flowed down through the uplands over which we drove, with a small volume that seemed quite inadequate to slake the wide drought of the landscape, in which, except for the cypresses about the villas, no tree lifted its head. There were not even olives; even the vineyards had vanished. The fields were green with well-started wheat, but of other husbandry there was scarcely a sign. Yet the peasants whom we met were well dressed (to be sure it was Sunday), and there was that air of comfort about the farmsteads which is seldom absent in Tuscany. All along the road were people going to vespers; and these people were often girls, young and pretty, who, with their arms about one another's waists, walked three and four abreast, the wide brims of their straw hats lifting round their faces like the disks of sunflowers. A great many of them were blonde; at least one in ten had blue eyes and red hair, and they must have been the far-descended children of those seigneurs and soldiers among whom Charlemagne portioned his Italian lands, marking to this day a clear distinction of race between the citizens and the contadini. By and by we came to a little country church, before which in the grassy piazza two men had a humble show of figs and cakes for sale in their wagon-beds, and another was selling wine by the glass from a heap of flasks on his stand. Here again I was reminded of Quebec, for the interior of this church was, in its bareness and poverty, quite like the poor little Huron village church at the Falls of Lorette.

Our drive was out from the Porta Pispini southward, and back to the city through the Porta Romana; but pleasure lies in any course you take, and perhaps greater pleasure in any other than this. The beauty of the scenery is wilder and ruggeder than at Florence. In the country round Siena all is free and open, with none of those high garden walls that baffle approach in the Florentine neighborhood. But it seems to have been as greatly loved and as much frequented, and there are villas and palaces everywhere, with signs of that personal eccentricity in the architecture and inscriptions for which the Italians ought to be as famous as the English. Out of the Porta Camollia, in the Palazzo del Diavolo, which was the scene of stirring facts during the great siege, when the Sienese once beat Duke Cosimo's Florentines out of it, the caprice of the owner has run riot in the decoration of the brick front, where heads of Turks and Saracens are everywhere thrusting out of the frieze and cornice. At Poggio Pini an inscription on the porter's lodge declares: "Count Casti de' Vecchi, jealous conservator of the ornaments of the above-situated villa Poggio Pini, his glory, his care, placed me guardian of this approach."

The pines thus tenderly and proudly watched would not strike the American as worthy so much anxiety; but perhaps they are so in a country which has wasted its whole patrimony of trees, as we are now so wickedly wasting ours. The variety of timber which one sees in Tuscany is very small: pines, poplars, oaks, walnuts, chestnuts, – that is the whole story of the forest growth. Its brevity impressed us particularly in our long drive to Belcaro, which I visited for its interest as the quarters of the Marquis of Marignano, the Imperialist general during the siege. Two cannon-balls imbedded in its walls recall the fight, with an appropriate inscription; but whether they were fired by Marignano while it was occupied by the Sienese, or by the Sienese after he took it, I cannot now remember. I hope the reader will not mind this a great deal, especially as I am able to offer him the local etymology of the name of Belcaro: *bel* because it is so beautiful, and *caro* because it cost so much. It is now owned by two brothers, rich merchants of Siena, one of whom lives in it, and it is approached through a landscape wild, and sometimes almost savage, like that all around Siena, but of more fertile aspect than that to the southward. The reader must always think of the wildness in Italy as different from our primeval wildness; it is the wildness of decay, of relapse. At one point a group of cypresses huddling about the armless statue of some poor god thrilled us with a note, like the sigh of a satyr's reed, from the antique world; at another, a certain wood-grown turn of the road, there was a brick stairway, which had once led to some pavilion of the hoop and bag-wig age, and now, grown with thick moss and long grasses, had a desolation more exquisite than I can express.

Belcaro itself, however, when we came to it, was in perfectly good repair, and afforded a satisfying image of a mediæval castle, walled and fossed about, and lifting its mighty curtains of masonry just above the smooth level of the ilex-tops that hedged it loftily in. There was not very much to see within it, except the dining-hall, painted by Peruzzi with the Judgment of Paris. After we had admired this we were shown across the garden to the little lodge which the same painter has deliciously frescoed with indecenter fables than any outside of the Palazzo del Tè at Mantua. Beside it is the chapel in which he has indifferently turned his hand, with the same brilliant facility, to the illustration of holy writ and legend. It was a curious civilization. Both lodge and chapel were extraordinarily bright and cheerful.

From these works of art we turned and climbed to the superb promenade which crowns the wide wall of the castle. In the garden below, a chilly bed of anemones blew in the March wind, and the top where we stood was swept by a frosty blast, while the waning sunshine cast a sad splendor over the city on her hill seven miles away. A delicate rose-light began to bathe it, in which the divine cathedral looked like some perfect shape of cloudland; while the clustering towers, palaces and gates, and the wandering sweep of the city wall seemed the details of a vision too lovely for waking eyes.

# Pitiless Pisa

## I.

As Pisa made no comment on the little changes she may have observed in me since we had last met, nineteen years before, I feel bound in politeness to say that I found her in April, 1883, looking not a day older than she did in December, 1864. In fact she looked younger, if anything, though it may have been the season that made this difference in her. She was in her spring attire, freshly, almost at the moment, put on; and that counts for much more in Pisa than one who knew her merely in the region of her palaces and churches and bridges would believe. She has not, indeed, quite that breadth of orchards and gardens within her walls which Siena has, but she has space enough for nature to flourish at ease there; and she has many deserted squares and places where the grass was sprouting vigorously in the crevices of the pavement. All this made her perceptibly younger, even with her memories running so far back of Roman times, into twilights whither perhaps a less careful modern historian than myself would not follow them. But when I am in a town that has real claims to antiquity, I like to allow them to the uttermost; and with me it is not merely

a duty, it is a pleasure, to remind the reader that Pisa was
founded by Pelops, the grandson of Jove, and the son of
Tantalus, king of Phrygia. He was the same who was slain
by his father, and served in a banquet to the gods, to try if
they knew everything, or could be tricked into eating of the
hideous repast; and it was after this curious experience –
Ceres came in from the field, very tired and hungry, and
popped down and tasted a bit of his shoulder before they
could stop her – that, being restored to life by his grandfather, he visited Italy, and, liking the situation at the mouth
of the Arno, built his city there. This is the opinion of
Pliny and Solinus, and that generally adopted by the Pisan
chroniclers; but the sceptical Strabo would have us think
that Pisa was not founded till much later, when Nestor,
sailing homeward after the fall of Troy, was cast away on
the Etruscan shore at this point. There are some historians
who reconcile the accounts by declaring that Nestor merely
joined the Phrygians at Pisa, and could never have pretended
to found the city. I myself incline to this notion; but even
if Pisa was not built till after the fall of Troy, the reader
easily perceives that a sense of her antiquity might affect an
Ohio man, even after a residence in Boston. A city founded
by Pelops or Nestor could not be converted to Christianity
by a less person than St. Peter, who, on his way to Rome,
was expressly wrecked on the Pisan coasts for that purpose.
Her faith, like her origin, is as ancient as possible, and Pisa
was one of the first Italian communities to emerge from
the ruin of the Roman Empire into a vigorous and splendid
life of her own. Early in the Middle Ages she had, with the
arrogance of long-established consequence, superciliously
explained the Florentines, to an Eastern potentate who had

just heard of them, as something like the desert Arabs, —
a lawless, marauding, barbarous race, the annoyance of all
respectable and settled communities. In those days Pisa had
not only commerce with the East, but wars; and in 1005 she
famously beat back the Saracens from their conquests in the
northern Mediterranean, and, after a struggle of eighteen
years, ended by carrying the war into Africa and capturing
Carthage with the Emir of the Saracens in it. In the beginning
of this war her neighbor Lucca, fifteen miles away, profited
by her preoccupation to attack her, and this is said to have
been one of the first quarrels, if not the first, in which the
Italian cities asserted their separate nationality and their independence of the empire. It is supposed on that account to
have been rather a useful event, though it is scarcely to be
praised otherwise. Of course the Pisans took it out of the
Lucchese afterwards in the intervals of their more important wars with the Genoese by sea and the Florentines by
land. There must have been fighting pretty well all the time,
back and forth across the vineyards and olive orchards that
stretch between the two cities; I have counted up eight distinct wars, bloody and tedious, in which they ravaged each
other's territory, and I dare say I have missed some. Once
the Pisane captured Lucca and sacked it, and once the Lucchese took Pisa and sacked it; the Pisans were Ghibelline,
and the Lucchese were Guelph, and these things had to be.
In the mean time, Pisa was waging, with varying fortune,
seven wars with Genoa, seven other with Florence, three
with Venice, and one with Milan, and was in a spirited state
of continual party strife within herself; though she found
leisure to take part in several of the crusades, to break the
naval supremacy of the Saracens, and to beat the Greeks in

sea-fights under the walls of Constantinople. The warlike passions of men were tightly wound up in those days, and Pisa was set to fight for five hundred years. Then she fell at last, in 1509, under the power of those upstart Florentines, whom she had despised so long.

Almost from the beginning of their rivalry, some three or four hundred years before, the triumph of Florence was a foregone conclusion. The serious historians are rather ashamed of the incident that kindled the first hostilities between the two cities but the chroniclers, who are still more serious, treat it with perfect gravity; and I, who am always with the chroniclers, cannot offer it less respect. The fact is, that one day, at the time of the coronation of the Emperor Frederick II. in Rome, the Florentine ambassador, who was dining with a certain cardinal, either politely or sincerely admired the cardinal's lapdog so much that the cardinal could not help making him a present of the dog, out of hand. The Florentine thought this extremely handsome of the cardinal, and the cardinal forgot all about it; so that when the Pisan ambassador came to dine with him the next day, and professed also to be charmed with this engaging lapdog, the cardinal promptly bestowed it upon him in his turn; nothing could equal the openhandedness of that cardinal in the matter of lapdogs. He seems to have forgotten his gift to the Pisan as readily as he had forgotten his present to the Florentine; or possibly he thought that neither of them would have the ill manners to take him in earnest; very likely it was the custom to say to a guest who admired your dog, "He is yours," and then think no more about it. However, the Florentine sent for the dog and got it, and then the Pisan sent, and got the poor cardinal's best excuses; one imagines the desolated smiles and deprecating shrugs with which he must have made them. The affair might have ended there, if it had not happened that a party of Florentines and a party of Pisans met shortly afterwards in Rome, and exchanging some natural jeers and taunts concerning the good cardinal's gift, came to blows about it. The Pisans were the first to begin this quarrel, and all the Florentines in Rome were furious. Oddo di Arrigo Fifanti, whom the diligent reader of these pages will remember as one of the Florentine gentlemen who helped cut the throat of Buondelmonte on his wedding day, chanced to be in Rome, and put himself at the head of the Florentines. He was not the kind of man to let any sort of quarrel suffer in his hands, and he led the Florentines on to attack the Pisan legation in the street.

When the news of this outrage came to Pisa, it set the hot little state in a flame. She was glad of a chance to break with Florence, for the Pisans had long been jealous of the growing power of the upstart city, and they hastened to make reprisal by seizing all the Florentine merchandise within their borders. Florence still remained in such awe of the old-established respectability of Pisa, and of her supremacy by land and sea, lately illustrated in her victorious wars with the Genoese and Saracens, that she was willing to offer any reasonable reparation; and her consuls even sent to pay secretly the price of the confiscated goods, if only they could have them back, and so make an appearance of honorable reconciliation before their people. The Pisan authorities refused these humble overtures, and the Florentines desperately prepared for war. The campaign ended in a single battle at Castel del Bosco, where the Florentines, supported by the Lucchese, defeated the Pisans with great slaughter, and conquered a peace that left them masters of the future. After that Pisa was in league with Florence, as she had been in league with her before that, against the encroachments of the emperors upon the liberties of the Tuscan cities, and she was often at war with her, siding with the Sienese in one of their famous defeats at the hands of the Florentines, and generally doing what she could to disable and destroy her rival. She seems to have grown more and more incapable of governing herself; she gave herself to this master and that; and at last, in 1406, after a siege of eight months, she was reduced by the Florentines. Her women had fought together with her men in her defence; the people were starving, and the victors wept at the misery they saw within the fallen city.

The Florentines had hoped to inherit the maritime greatness of Pisa, but this perished with her; thereafter the ships that left her famous arsenal were small and few. The Florentines treated their captive as well as a mediæval people knew how, and addressed themselves to the restoration of her prosperity; but she languished in their hold for nearly a hundred years, when Pietro de' Medici, hoping to make interest for himself with Charles VIII. of France (who seems to have invaded Italy rather for the verification of one of Savonarola's prophecies than for any other specific purpose), handed over Pisa with the other Florentine fortresses to the French troops. When their commandant evacuated the place, he restored it not to the Florentines but to the Pisans. The Florentines set instantly and actively about the reconquest, and after a siege and a blockade that lasted for years, they accomplished it. In this siege, as in the other great defence, the Pisan women fought side by side with the men; it is told of two sisters working upon the fortifications, that when one was killed by a cannon-shot the other threw her body into a gabion, covered it with earth, and went on with her work above it. Before Pisa fell people had begun to drop dead of famine in her streets, and the Florentines, afraid that they would destroy the city in their despair, offered them terms far beyond their hopes, after a war of fifteen years.

## II.

What is old in the history of Pisa is that it has given but one name to common remembrance. Her prosperity was early and great, and her people employed it in the cultivation of all the arts; yet Andrea and Nicolo Pisano are almost the only artists whose fame is associated with that of their native city. She was perpetually at war by sea and by land, yet her admirals and generals are unknown to the world. Her university is one of the oldest and most learned in Italy, yet she produced no eminent scholars or poets, and one hardly realizes that the great Galileo, who came a century after the fall of his country, was not a Florentine but a Pisan by birth; he was actually of a Florentine family settled in Pisa. When one thinks of Florence, one thinks of Dante, of Giotto, of Cimabue, of Brunelleschi, of Michelangelo, of Savonarola, and of Lorenzo de' Medici and Leo X., of Boccaccio and Pulci and Politian, of Machiavellli, of Giovanni delle Bande Nere and Gino Capponi, of Guido Cavalcanti, of Amerigo Vespucci, of Benvennto Cellini, and Masaccio and Botticelli, and all the rest. When one thinks of Siena, one thinks of St.

Catharine, and Ochino, and Socinus, and the Piccolomini, and Bandini, and Sodoma; but when one thinks of Pisa, Ugolino is the sole name that comes into one's mind. I am not at all sure, however, that one ought to despise Pisa for her lack of celebrities; I am rather of a contrary opinion. It is certain that such a force and splendor as she was for five hundred years could have been created only by a consensus of mighty wills, and it seems to me that a very pretty case might be made out in behalf of the democracy whose level was so high that no one head could be seen above it. Perhaps this is what we are coming to in our own civilization, and I am disposed to take heart from the heroless history of Pisa when I look round over the vast plain of our equality, where every one is as great as every other.

I wish, if this is the case, we might come finally to anything as clean and restful and lovely as I found Pisa on the day of my arrival; but of course that would be much more difficult for a continent than for a city, and probably our last state will not be so pleasant. On our way down from Florence, through much the same landscape as that through which we had started to Siena, the peach-trees were having their turn in the unhurried Italian spring's succession of blossoms, and the fields were lit with their pathetic pink, where earlier the paler bloom of the almond had prevailed. As I said, Pisa herself was in her spring dress, and it may be that the season had touched her with the langour which it makes the whole world feel, as she sat dreaming beside her Arno, in the midst of the gardens that compassed her about within her walls. I do not know what Pisa had to say to other tourists who arrived that day, but we were old friends, and she regarded me with a frank, sad wonder when she read in my eyes a determination to take notes of her.

"Is it possible?" she expressed, with that mute, melancholy air of hers. "You, who have lived in Italy, and ought to know better? You, who have been here, before? Sit down with me beside the Arno!" and she indicated two or three empty bridges, which I was welcome to, or if I preferred half a mile or so of that quay, which has the noblest sweep in the world, there it was, vacant for me. I shrugged my excuses, as well as I could, and indicated the artist at my side, who with his etching-plate under his arm, and his hat in his hand, was making his manners to Pisa, and I tried to explain that we were both there under contract to produce certain illustrated papers for *The Century*.

"What papers? What Century?" she murmured, and tears came into the eyes of the beautiful ghost; and she added with an inexpressible pathos and bitterness, "I remember no century, since the fifteenth, when – I – died."

She would not say, when she fell under the power of her enemy, but we knew she was thinking of Florence; and as she bowed her face in her hands, we turned away with our hearts in our throat.

We thought it well not to go about viewing the monuments of her fallen grandeur at once, – they are all kept in wonderful repair, – and we left the Arno, whose mighty curve is followed on either side by lines of magnificent palaces, and got our driver to carry us out to the streets that dwindled into lanes beside the gardens fenced in by the red brick city walls. At one point a long stretch of the wall seemed trellised for yellow roses which covered acres of it with their golden multitude; but when we got down and

walked nearer, with the permission of the peasant whose
field we passed through, we found they were lemons. He
said they grew very well in that shelter and exposure, and
his kind old weather-beaten, friendly face was almost the
color of one. He bade us go anywhere we liked in his garden, and he invited us to drink of the water of his well,
which he said never went dry in the hottest weather. Then
he returned to his fat old wife, who had kept on weeding,
and bent down beside her and did not follow us for drink-
money, but returned a self-respectful adieu from a distance,
when we called a good-by before getting into our carriage.
We generalized from his behavior a manly independence of
character in the Pisan people, and I am sure we were not
mistaken in the beauty of the Pisan women, who, as we met
them in the street, were all extremely pretty, and young,
many of them, even after five hundred years. One gets over
expecting good looks in Tuscany; and perhaps this was the
reason why we prized the loveliness of the Pisans. It may
have been comparative, only, though I am inclined to think
it was positive. At any rate, there can be no doubt about
the landscape outside the walls, which we drove into a little
way out of one of the gates, to return by another. It was a
plain country, and at this point a line of aqueduct stretched
across the smiling fields to the feet of the arid, purple hills,
that propped the blue horizon. There was something richly
simple in the elements of the picture, which was of as few
tones as a landscape of Titian or Raphael, and as strictly
subordinated in its natural features to the human interest,
which we did our best to represent. I dare say our best was
but poor. Every acre of that plain had been the theatre of
a great tragedy; every rood of ground had borne its hero.

Now, in the advancing spring, the grass and wheat were long enough to flow in the wind, and they flowed like the ripples of a wide green sea to the feet of those purple hills, away from our feet where we stood beside our carriage on its hither shore. The warmth of the season had liberated the fine haze that dances above the summer fields, and this quivered before us like the confluent phantoms of multitudes, indistinguishably vast, who had fallen there in immemorial strife. But we could not stand musing long upon this fact; we had taken that carriage by the hour. Yet we could not help loitering along by the clear stream that followed the road, till it brought us to a flour-whitened mill, near the city wall, slowly and thoughtfully turning its huge undershot wheel; and I could not resist entering and speaking to the miller, where, leaning upon a sack of wheat, he dimly loomed through the powdered air, in the exact attitude of a miller I used to know in a mill on the Little Miami, in Ohio, when I was a boy.

### III.

I try to give the reader a true impression of the sweet confusion of travel in those old lands. In the phrases that come out of the point of the pen, rather than out of the head or the heart, we talk about losing ourselves in the associations of the past; but we never do it. A prime condition of our sympathy with it, is that we always and every instant and vividly find our dreary, tiresome, unstoried, unstoriable selves in it; and if I had been less modern, less recent, less raw, I should have been by just so much indifferent to the antique charm of the place. In the midst of my reverie of the Pisan past, I dreamily asked the miller about the milling business in the Pisan present. I forget what he said.

The artist outside had begun an etching, – if you let that artist out of your sight half a second he began an etching, – and we got back by a common effort into the town again, where we renewed our impression of a quiet that was only equalled by its cleanliness, of a cleanliness that was only surpassed by its quiet. I think of certain dim arcaded streets; of certain genial, lonely, irregular squares, more or less planted with pollarded sycamores, just then woolily tufted with their leaf-buds; and I will ask the reader to think of such white light over all as comes in our own first real spring days; for in some atmospheric qualities and effects the spring is nowhere so much alike as in America and Italy. In one of these squares the boys were playing ball, striking it with a small tambourine instead of a bat; in another, some young girls sat under a sycamore with their sewing; and in a narrow street running out of this was the house where Galileo was born. He is known to have said that the world moves; but I do not believe it has moved much in that neighborhood since his time. His natal roof is overlooked by a lofty gallery leading into Prince Corsini's garden; and I wish I could have got inside of that garden; it must have been pleasanter than the street in which Galileo was born, and which more nearly approached squalor in its condition than any other street that I remember in Pisa. It had fallen from no better state, and must always have witnessed to the poverty of the decayed Florentine family from which Galileo sprang.

I left the artist there – beginning an etching as usual – and wandered back to our hotel; for it was then in the drowsy heart of the late afternoon, and I believed that Pisa had done

all that she could for me in one day. But she had reserved a
little surprise, quaint and unimaginable enough, in a small
chapel of the Chiesa Evangelica Metodista Italiana, which she
suddenly showed me in a retired street I wandered through.
This Italian Evangelical Methodist Church was but a tiny
structure, and it stood back from the street in a yard, with
some hollies and myrtles before it, – simple and plain, like
a little Methodist church at home. It had not a frequented
look, and I was told afterwards that the Methodists of Pisa
were in that state of arrest which the whole Protestant
movement in Italy has fallen into, after its first vigorous
impulse. It has not lost ground, but it has not gained, which
is also a kind of loss. Apparently the Protestant church which
prospers best in Italy is the ancient Italian church of the
Waldenses. This presents the Italians a Protestantism of their
own invention, while perhaps the hundred religions which
we offer them are too distracting, if unaccompanied by our
one gravy. It is said that our missionaries have unexpected
difficulties to encounter in preaching to the Italians, who are
not amused, as we should be, by a foreigner's blunder, in our
language, but annoyed and revolted by incorrect Italian from
the pulpit. They have, moreover, their intellectual pride in
the matter: they believe that if Protestantism had been the
wiser and better thing we think it, the Italians would have
found it out long ago for themselves. As it is, such proselytes
as we make are among the poor and ignorant; though that
is the way all religions begin.

After the Methodist church it was not at all astonishing to
come upon an agricultural implement warehouse – alongside of a shop glaring with alabaster statuary – where the
polite attendant offered me an American pump as the very

best thing of its kind that I could use on my *podere*. When I explained that I and his pump were fellow-countrymen, I could see that we both rose in his respect. A French pump, he said, was not worth anything in comparison, and I made my own inferences as to the relative inferiority of a French man.


## IV.

When I got to the hotel I asked for the key to my room, which opened by an inner door into the artist's room, and was told that the artist had it. He had come out by that door, it appeared, and carried off the key in his pocket.

"Very well," I said, "then let us get in with the porter's key."

They answered that the porter had no key, and they confessed that there was no other key than that which my friend had in his pocket. They maintained that for one door one key was enough, and they would not hear to the superiority of the American hotel system of several keys, which I, flown with pride by the lately acknowledged pre-eminence of American pumps, boasted for their mortification. I leave the sympathetic reader of forty-six to conceive the feelings of a man whose whole being had set nap-wards in a lethal tide, and who now found himself arrested and as it were dammed up in inevitable vigils. In the reading-room there were plenty of old newspapers that one could sleep over; but there was not a lounge, not an arm-chair. I pulled up one of the pitiless, straightbacked seats to the table, and meditated upon the lost condition of an artist who, without even meaning it, could be so wicked; and then I opened the hotel register in which the different guests had inscribed their names, their residences, their feelings, their opinions of Pisa and of the Hotel Minerva.

"This," I said to my bitter heart, "will help a man to sleep, standing upright."

But to my surprise I presently found myself interested in these predecessors of mine. They were, in most unexpected number, South Americans, and there were far more Spanish than English names from our hemisphere, though I do not know why the South Americans should not travel as well as we of the Northern continent. There were, of course, Europeans of all races and languages, conspicuous among whom for their effusion and expansiveness were the French. I should rather have thought the Germans would be foremost in this sort, but these French bridal couples – they all seemed to be on their wedding journeys – let their joy bubble frankly out in the public record. One Baron – declared that he saw Pisa for the second time, and "How much more beautiful it is," he cries, "now when I see it on my bridal tour!" and his wife writes fondly above this, – one fancies her with her left arm thrown round his neck while they bend over the book together, – "Life is a journey which we should always make in pairs." On another page, "Cecie and Louis –, on their wedding journey, are very content with this hotel, and still more with being together."

Who could they have been, I wonder; and are they still better satisfied with each other's company than with the hotels they stop at?

The Minerva was a good hotel; not perhaps all that these Gallic doves boasted it, but very fair indeed, and the landlord took off a charge for two pigeons when we represented that he had only given us one for dinner. The artist came in, after a while, with the appetite of a good conscience, and that dinner almost starved us. We tried to eke out the pigeon with vegetables, but the cook's fire had gone down, and we could get nothing but salad. There is nothing I hate more, under such circumstances, than a *giardinetto* for dessert, and a gardenette was all we had; a little garden that grew us only two wizened pears, some dried prunes, and two slices of Gruyère cheese, fitter for a Parisian bridal pair than for us. If my memory serves me right we had to go out to a café for our after-dinner coffee.

At any rate we went out, and walked up to look at the Arno under the pale moon. We found the river roughed by the chill wind that flared the line of lamps defining the curve of the quay before the shadowy palaces, and swept through the quiet streets, and while we lounged upon the parapet, a poor mountebank – of those that tumble for *centesimi* before the cafés – came by, shivering and shrinking in his shabby tights. His spangled breech-cloth emitted some forlorn gleams; he was smoking a cigarette, and trying to keep on by a succession of shrugs the jacket that hung from one of his shoulders. I give him to the reader for whatever he can do with him in an impression of Pisa.

## V.

One of our first cares in Pisa was of course to visit the Four Fabrics, as the Italians call, *par excellence*, the Duomo, the Leaning Tower, the Baptistery, and the Campo Santo. I say cares, for to me it was not a great pleasure. I perceive, by reference to my notebook, that I found that group far less

impressive than at first, and that the Campo Santo especially
appeared conscious and finicking. I had seen those Orgagna
frescos before, and I had said to myself twenty years ago,
in obedience to whatever art-critic I had in my pocket,
that here was the highest evidence of the perfect sincerity
in which the early masters wrought, – that no one could
have painted those horrors of death and torments of hell
who had not thoroughly believed in them. But this time
I had my doubts, and I questioned if the painters of the
Campo Santo might not have worked with almost as little
faith and reverence as so many American humorists. Why
should we suppose that the men who painted the Vergognosa
peeping through her fingers at the debauch of Noah should
not be capable of making ferocious fun of the scenes which
they seemed to depict seriously? There is, as we all know,
a modern quality in the great minds, the quickest wits,
of all ages, and I do not feel sure these old painters are
always to be taken at their word. Were they not sometimes
making a mock of the devout clerics and laics who employed
them? It is bitter fun, I allow. The Death and the Hell of
Orgagna are atrocious – nothing less. A hideous fancy, if
not a grotesque, insolent humor, riots through those scenes,
where the damned are shown with their entrails dangling
out (my pen cannot be half so plain as his brush), with their
arms chopped off, and their tongues torn out by fiends, with
their women's breasts eaten by snakes. I for one will not
pretend to have revered those works of art, or to have felt
anything but loathing in their presence. If I am told that
I ought at least to respect the faith with which the painter
wrought, I say that faith was not respectable; and I can honor
him more if I believe he was portraying those evil dreams

in contempt of them, — doing what he could to make faith
in them impossible by realizing them in all the details of
their filthy cruelty. It was misery to look upon them, and it
was bliss to turn my back and give my gaze to the innocent
wilding flowers and weeds, — the daisies that powdered the
sacred earth brought from the Holy Land in the Pisan galleys
of old, for the sweeter repose of those laid away here to
wait the judgment day. How long they had been sleeping
already! But they do not dream; that was one comfort.

I revisited the Baptistery for the sake of the famous echo
which I had heard before, and which had sweetly lingered
in my sense all these twenty years. But I was now a little
disappointed in it, — perhaps because the custodian who had
howled so skilfully to evoke it was no longer there, but a
mere tyro intent upon his half franc, with no real feeling for
ululation as an art. Guides and custodians of an unexampled
rapacity swarmed in and all about the Four Fabrics, and
beggars, whom we had almost forgotten in Florence, were
there in such number that if the Leaning Tower were to
fall, as it still looks capable of doing at any moment, it
would half depopulate Pisa. I grieve to say that I encouraged
mendicancy in the person of an old woman whom I gave a
franc by mistake for a soldo. She had not the public spirit to
refuse it; without giving me time to correct the error, her
hand closed upon it like a talon of a vulture, and I had to get
what consolation I could out of pretending to have meant
to give her a franc, and to take lightly the blessings under
which I really staggered.

It may have been this misadventure that cast a malign
light upon the cathedral, which I found, after that of Siena,
not at all estimable. I dare say it had its merits; but I could

get no pleasure even out of the swinging lamp of Galileo;
it was a franc, large as the full moon, and reproachfully
pale, that waved to and fro before my eyes. This cathedral,
however, is only the new Duomo of Pisa, being less than
eight hundred years of age, and there is an old Duomo,
in another part of the city, which went much more to my
heart. I do not pretend that I entered it; but it had a lovely
façade of Pisan gothic, mellowed through all its marble
by the suns of a thousand summers, and weed-grown in
every neglected niche and nook where dust and seeds could
be lodged; so that I now wonder I did not sit down before
it and spend the rest of my life there.

## VI.

The reader, who has been requested to imagine the irregular form and the perpetually varying heights and depths
of Siena, is now set the easier task of supposing Pisa shut
within walls almost quadrangular, and reposing on a level
which expands to the borders of the hills beyond Lucca,
and drops softly with the Arno towards the sea. The river
divides the southward third of the city from the rest, to
which stately bridges bind it again. The group of the Four
Fabrics, to which we have paid a *devoir* tempered by modern
misgiving, rises in aristocratic seclusion in the northwest-
ern corner of the quadrangle, and the outer wall of the
Campo Santo is the wall of the city. Nothing statelier than
the position of these edifices could be conceived; and yet
their isolation, so favorable to their reproduction in small
alabaster copies, costs them something of the sympathy of
the sensitive spectator. He cannot withhold his admiration

of that grandeur, but his soul turns to the Duomo in the busy heart of Florence, or to the cathedral, pre-eminent but not solitary in the crest of Siena. The Pisans have put their famous group apart from their streets and shops, and have consecrated to it a region which no business can take them to. In this they have gained distinction and effect for it, but they have lost for it that character of friendly domesticity which belongs to all other religious edifices that I know in Italy. Here, as in some other things not so easily definable, the people so mute in all the arts but architecture — of which they were the origin and school in Italy — seem to have expressed themselves mistakenly. The Four Fabrics are where they are to be seen, to be visited, to be wondered at; but they are remote from human society, and they fail of the last and finest effect of architecture, — the perfect adaptation of houses to the use of men. Perhaps also one feels a want of unity in the group; perhaps they are too much like dishes set upon the table: the Duomo a vast and beautiful pudding; the Baptistery a gigantic *charlotte russe;* the Campo Santo an exquisite structure in sugar; the Leaning Tower, a column of ice-cream which has been weakened at the base by too zealous an application of hot water to the outside of the mould. But I do not insist upon this comparison; I only say that I like the ancient church of St. Paul by the Arno. Some question whether it was really the first cathedral of Pisa, maintaining that it was merely used as such while the Duomo was in repair after the fire from which it suffered shortly after its completion.

One must nowadays seem to have some preference in all æsthetic matters, but the time was when polite tourists took things more easily. In the seventeenth century, "Richard Lassels, Gent. who Travelled through Italy five times as

Tutor to several of the English Nobility and Gentry," says of the Pisan Duomo that it "is a neat Church for structure, and for its three Brazen Doors historied with a fine Basso rilievo. It's built after *La maniera Tedescha*, a fashion of Building much used in Italy four or five hundred years ago, and brought in by Germans or Tedeschi, saith Vasari. Near to the Domo stands (if leaning may be called standing) the bending Tower, so artificially made, that it seems to be falling, and yet it stands firm. . . . On the other side of the Domo, is the Campo Santo, a great square cloistered about with a low cloister curiously painted."

Here is no trouble of mind about the old masters, either architects or painters, but a beautiful succinctness, a tranquil brevity, which no concern for the motives, or meanings, or aspirations of either penetrates. We have taken upon ourselves in these days a heavy burden of inquiry as to what the mediæval masters thought and felt; but the tourist of the seventeenth century could say of the Pisan Duomo that it was "a neat church for structure," and of the Campo Santo that it was "curiously painted," and there an end. Perhaps there was a relief for the reader also in this method. Master Lassels vexed himself to spell his Italian correctly no more than he did his English.

He visited, apparently with more interest, the Church of the Knights of St. Stephen, which indeed I myself found full of unique attraction. Of these knights he says: "They wear a Red Cross of Satin upon their Cloaks, and profess to fight against the Turks. For this purpose they have here a good House and Maintainance. Their Church is beautified without with a handsome Faciata of White Marble, and within with Turkish Ensigns and divers Lanterns of Capitanesse Gallics. In this House the Knights live in common, and they are well maintained. In their Treasury they shew a great Buckler of Diamonds, won in a Battle against the Turks. . . . They have their Cancellarla, a Catalogue of those Knights who have done notable service against the Turks, which serves for a powerful exhortation to their Successors, to do, and die bravely. In fine, these Knights may marry if they will, and live in their own particular houses, but many of them choose celibate, as more convenient for brave Soldiers; Wives and Children being the true *impedimenta exercitus.*"

The knights were long gone from their House and Maintenance in 1883, and I suspect it is years since any of them even professed to fight the Turks. But their church is still there, with their trophies, which I went and admired; and I do not know that there is anything in Pisa which gives you a more vivid notion of her glory in the past than those flags taken from the infidels and those carvings that once enriched her galleys. These and the ship-yards by the Arno, from which her galleys were launched, do really recall the majesty and dominion of the sea which once was hers — and then Genoa's, and then Venice's, and then the Hanseatic Cities', and then Holland's, and then England's; and shall be ours when the Moral Force of the American Navy is appreciated. At present Pisa and the United States are equally formidable as maritime powers, unless indeed this conveys too strong an impression of the decay of Pisa.

## VII.

Issuing from the Church of the Cavaliers I found myself in the most famous spot in the whole city: the wide dusty square where the Tower of Famine once stood, and where you may still see a palace with iron baskets swung from the corners of the façade, in which it is said the wicked Archbishop Ruggieri used to put the heads of traitors. It may not be his palace, and the baskets may not have been used for this purpose; but there is no doubt that this was the site of the tower, which was not demolished till 1655, and that here it was that Ugolino and his children and grandchildren cruelly perished.

The writer of an excellent little local guide to Pisa, which I bought on my first visit, says that Dante has told the story of Count Ugolino della Gherardesca, and that "after Dante, God alone can repeat it." Yet I fancy the tragedy will always have a fascination to the scribbler who visits Pisa, irresistibly tempting him to recall it to his reader. I for my part shall not do less than remind him that Ugolino was Captain of the People and Podestà of Pisa at the time of her great defeat by Genoa in 1284, when so many of her best and bravest were carried off prisoners that a saying arose, "If you want to see Pisa, go to Genoa." In those days they had a short and easy way of accounting for disaster, which has been much practised since down even to the date of our own civil war; they attributed it to treason, and in this case they were pretty clear that Count Ugolino was the traitor. He sailed away with his squadron before his critics thought the day lost; and after the battle, in his negotiations with Florence and Genoa they declared that he behaved as only a man would who wished to ruin his country in order to rule her. He had already betrayed his purpose of founding an hereditary lordship in Pisa, as the Visconti had done in Milan and the Scaligeri in Verona, and to this end had turned Guelph from being ancestrally Ghibelline; for his name is one of the three still surviving in

Tuscany of the old German nobility founded there by the
emperors. He was a man of furious and ruthless temper; he
had caused one of his nephews to be poisoned, he stabbed
another, and when the young man's friend, a nephew of the
Archbishop, would have defended him, Ugolino killed him
with his own hand. The Archbishop, as a Ghibelline, was
already no friend of Ugolino's, and here now was bloodshed
between them. "And what happened to Count Ugolino a
little after," says the Florentine chronicler, Villani, "was
prophesied by a wise and worthy man of the court, Marco
Lombardo; for when the count was chosen by all to be Lord
of Pisa, and when he was in his highest estate and felicity,
he made himself a splendid birthday feast, where he had his
children and grandchildren and all his lineage, kinsmen and
kinswomen, with great pomp of apparel, and ornament, and
preparation for a rich banquet. The count took this Marco,
and went about showing him his possessions and splendor,
and the preparation for the feast, and that done, he said,
'What do you think of it, Marco?' The sage answered at
once, and said, 'You are fitter for evil chance than any
baron of Italy.' And the count, afraid of Marco's meaning,
asked, 'Why?' And Marco answered, 'Because you lack
nothing but the wrath of God.' And surely the wrath of
God quickly fell upon him, as it pleased God, for his sins
and treasons; for as it had been intended by the Archbishop
of Pisa and his party to drive out of Pisa Nino and his
followers, and betray and entrammel Ugolino, and weaken
the Guelphs, the Archbishop ordered Count Ugolino to be
undone, and immediately set the people on in their fury to
attack and take his palace, giving the people to understand
that he had betrayed Pisa, and surrendered their castles to

the Florentines and Lucchese; and finding the people upon him, without hope of escape, Ugolino gave himself up, and in this assault his bastard son and one of his grandchildren were killed; and Ugolino being taken, and two of his sons and two of his son's sons, they threw them in prison, and drove his family and his followers out of Pisa. . . . The Pisans, who had thrown in prison Ugolino and his two sons, and two sons of his son Count Guelfo, as we have before mentioned, in a tower on the Piazza degli Anziani, caused the door of the tower to be locked and the keys to be thrown into the Arno, and forbidding these captives all food, in a few days they perished of hunger. But first, the count imploring a confessor, they would not allow him a friar or priest that he might confess. And all five being taken out of the tower together, they were vilely buried; and from that time the prison was called the Tower of Famine, and will be so always. For this cruelty the Pisans were strongly blamed by the whole world, wherever it was known, not so much for the count, who for his crimes and treasons was perhaps worthy of such a death, but for his sons and grandsons, who were young, boys, and innocent; and this sin, committed by the Pisans, did not remain unpunished, as may be seen in after time."

A monograph on Ugolino by an English writer states that the victims were rolled in the matting of their prison floor and interred, with the irons still on their limbs, in the cloister of the church of San Francesco. The grave was opened in the fourteenth century, and the irons taken out; again, in 1822, the remains were found and carelessly thrown together in a spot marked by a stone bearing the name of Vannuchi. Of the prison where they suffered, no more remains now than of the municipal eagles which the Republic put to moult there, and from which it was called the Moulting Tower before it was called the Tower of Famine.

## VIII.

The memory of that curious literary conjunction which once took place at Pisa, when Byron, Shelley, and Leigh Hunt met there to establish an English review on Italian ground, imparts to the old city an odor, faint now and very vague, of the time when Romance was new enough to seem immortal; but I could do little with this association, as an element of my impression. They will point you out, if you wish, the palace in which Byron lived on the Lung' Arno, but as I would not have gone to look at a palace with Byron alive in it, I easily excused myself for not hunting up this one of the residences with which he left Italy swarming. The Shelleys lived first in a villa, four miles off under the hills, but were washed out of it in one of the sudden inundations of the country, and spent the rest of their sojourn in the city, where Shelley alarmed his Italian friends by launching on the Arno in a boat he had contrived of pitched canvas and lath. His companion in this perilous navigation was that Mr. Williams with whom he was afterwards drowned in Spezzia Bay. "Once," writes Mrs. Shelley, "I went down with him to the mouth of the Arno, where the stream, then high and swift, met the tideless sea and disturbed its sluggish waters. It was a waste and dreary scene; the desert sand stretched into a point surrounded by waves that broke idly but perpetually around."

At Pisa there is nothing of this wildness or strife in the Arno, not so much as at Florence, where it rushes and brawls down its channel and over its dams and ripples. Its waters are turbid, almost black, but smooth, and they slip oilily away with many a wreathing eddy, round the curve of the magnificent quay, to which my mind recurs still as the noblest thing in Pisa; as the noblest thing, indeed, that any city has done with its river. But what quick and sensitive allies of Nature the Italians have always shown themselves! No suggestion of hers has been thrown away on them; they have made the most of her lavish kindness, and transmuted it into the glory and the charm of art. Our last moments of sight-seeing in Pisa were spent in strolling beside the river, in hanging on the parapet and delighting in the lines of that curve.

At one end of the city, before this begins, near a spick-and-span new iron bridge, is the mediæval tower of the galley prison, which we found exquisitely picturesque in the light of our last morning; and then, stretching up towards the heart of the town from this tower, were the ship-yards, with the sheds in which the old republic built the galleys she launched on every sea then known. They are used now for military stables; they are not unlike the ordinary horse-car stables of our civilization; and the grooms, swabbing the legs of the horses and combing their manes, were naturalized to our homesick sympathies by the homely community of their functions with those I had so often stopped to admire in my own land. There is no doubt but the toilet of a horse is something that interests every human being.

# Industrious Lucca

With rather less than the ordinary stupidity of tourists, wretched slaves of routine as they are, we had imagined the possibility of going to Lucca overland; that is, of driving fifteen miles across the country instead of taking the train. It would be as three hours against twenty minutes, and as fifteen francs against two; but my friend was young and I was imprudent, and we boldly ventured upon the expedition. I have never regretted it, which is what can be said of, alas, how few pleasures! On the contrary, it is rapture to think of it still.

Already, at eight o'clock of the April morning, the sun had filled the city with a sickening heat, which intimated pretty clearly what it might do for Pisa in August; but when we had mounted superbly to our carriage-seats, after pensioning all the bystanders, and had driven out of the city into the green plain beyond the walls, we found it a delicious spring day, warm, indeed, but full of a fervent life.

We had issued from the gate nearest the Four Fabrics, and I advise the reader to get that view of them if he can. To the backward glance of the journeyer toward Lucca, they

have the unity, the *ensemble*, the want of which weakens
their effect to proximity. Beside us swept the great level
to the blue-misted hills on our right; before us it stretched
indefinitely. From the grass, the larks were quivering up to
the perfect heaven, and the sympathy of Man with the tender
and lovely mood of Nature was expressed in the presence
of the hunters with their dogs, who were exploring the
herbage in quest of something to kill.

Perhaps I do man injustice. Perhaps the rapture of the
blameless *litterateur* and artist, who drove along crying out
over the exquisite beauty of the scene, was more justly
representative of our poor race. I am vexed now, when I
think how brief this rapture was, and how much it might
have been prolonged if we had bargained with our driver
to go slow. We had bargained for everything else; but who
could have imagined that one Italian could ever have been
fast enough for two Americans? He was even too fast. He
had a just pride in his beast, – as tough as the iron it was
the color of, – and when implored, in the interest of natural
beauty, not to urge it on, he misunderstood; he boasted
that it could keep up that pace all day, and he incited it
in the good Tuscan of Pisa to go faster yet. Ah me! What
enchanting villas he whirled us by! What gray chateaux!
What old wayside towers, hoary out of all remembrance!
What delightfully stupid-looking little stony picturesque
villages, in every one of which that poor artist and I would
have been glad to spend the whole day! But the driver could
not snatch the broad and constant features of the landscape
from us so quickly; these we had time to peruse and imprint
forever on our memories: the green expanses, the peach-
trees pink in their bloom; the plums and cherries putting on

their bridal white; the gray road, followed its whole length by the vines trained from trees to tall stakes across a space which they thus embowered continuously from field to field. Everywhere the peasants were working the soil; spading, not plowing their acres, and dressing it to the smoothness of a garden. It looked rich and fertile, and the whole land wore an air of smiling prosperity which I cannot think it put on expressly for us.

Pisa seemed hardly to have died out of the horizon before her ancient enemy began to rise from the other verge, beyond the little space in which they used to play bloodily at national hostilities. The plain narrowed as we approached, and hills hemmed us in on three sides, with snow-capped heights in the background, from which the air blew cooler and cooler. It was only eleven o'clock, and we would gladly have been all day on the road. But we pretended to be pleased with the mistaken zeal that had hurried us; it was so amiable, we could not help it; and we entered Lucca with the smiling resolution to make the most of it.

## II.

Lucca lies as flat as Pisa, but in shape it is as regularly oblong as that is square, and instead of the brick wall, which we had grown fond of there and in Siena, it has a girdle of gray stone, deeply moated without, and broadly levelled on top, where a lovely driveway winds round the ancient town. The wall juts in a score of angles, and the projecting spaces thus formed are planted with groups of forest trees, lofty and old, and giving a charm to the promenade exquisitely wild and rare.

To our approach, the clustering city towers and roofs promised a picturesqueness which she kept in her own fashion when we drove in through her gates, and were set down, after a dramatic rattling and hanging through her streets, at the door of the Universo, or the Croce di Malta, – I do not really remember which hotel it was. But I remember very well the whole domestic force of the inn seemed to be concentrated in the distracted servant who gave us our rooms, and was landlord, porter, accountant, waiter, and chambermaid all in one. It was an inn apparently very little tainted by tourist custom, and Lucca is certainly one of the less discovered of the Tuscan cities. At the *table d'hôte* in the evening our commensals were all Italians except an ancient English couple, who had lived so long in that region that they had rubbed off everything English but their speech. I wondered a good deal who they could be; they spoke conservatively – the foreigners are always conservative in Italy – of the good old ducal days of Lucca, when she had her own mild little despot, and they were now going to the Baths of Lucca to place themselves for the summer. They were types of a class which is numerous all over the continent, and which seems thoroughly content with expatriation. The Europeanized American is always apologetic; he says that America is best, and he pretends that he is going back there; but the continentalized Englishman has apparently no intention of repatriating himself. He has said to me frankly in one instance that England was beastly. But I own I should not like to have said it to him.

In their talk of the ducal past of Lucca these English people struck again the note which my first impression of Lucca had sounded. Lucca was a sort of republic for nearly a thousand years, with less interruption from lords, bishops, and foreign dominions than most of her sister commonwealths, and she kept her ancient liberties down to the time of the French revolution – four hundred years longer than Pisa, and two hundred and fifty years longer than Florence and Siena; as long, in fact, as Venice, which she resembled in an arbitrary change effected from a democratic to an aristocratic constitution at the moment when the change was necessary to her existence as an independent state. The duchy of Lucca created by the Congress of Vienna, 1817, and assigned to the Bourbons of Parma, lasted only thirty years, when it was merged by previous agreement in the grand duchy of Tuscany, the Bourbons going back to Parma, in which Napoleon's Austrian widow had meantime enjoyed a life interest. In this brief period, however, the old republican city assumed so completely the character of a little principality, that in spite of the usual Via Garibaldi and Corso Vittorio Emanuele, I could not banish the image of the ducal state from my mind. Yet I should be at a loss how to impart this feeling to every one, or to say why a vast dusty square, planted with pollarded sycamores, and a huge, ugly palace with but a fairish gallery of pictures, fronting upon the dust and sycamores, should have been so expressive of a ducal residence. There was a statue of Maria Louisa, the first ruler of the temporary duchy, in the midst of these sycamores, and I had a persistent whimsey of her reviewing her little ducal army there, as I sat and looked out from the open door of the restaurant where my friend and I were making the acquaintance of a number of strange dishes and trying our best to be friends with the Lucchese conception of a beefsteak.

It was not because I had no other periods to choose
from; in Lucca you can be overwhelmed with them. Her
chronicles do not indeed go back into the mists of fable for
her origin, but they boast an Etruscan, a Roman antiquity
which is hardly less formidable. Here in A. U. 515 there
was fixed a colony of two thousand citizens; here in 698
the great Cæsar met with Pompey and Crassus, and settled
who should rule in Rome. After the Romans, she knew the
Goths, the Lombards, and the Franks; then she had her own
tyrants, and in the twelfth century she began to have her own
consuls, the magistrates of her people's choice, and to have
her wars within and without, to be torn with faction and
menaced with conquest in the right Italian fashion. Once she
was sacked by the Pisans under the terrible Uguccione della
Fagginola, in 1314; and more than once she was sold. She
was sold for thirty-five thousand florins to two ambitious and
enterprising gentlemen, the Rossi brothers, of Parma, who,
however, were obliged to relinquish her to the Scaligeri of
Verona. This was the sorrow and shame that fell upon her
after a brief fever of conquest and glory, brought her by the
greatest of her captains, the famous Castruccio Castracani,
the condottiere, whose fierce, death-white face, bordered
by its pale yellow hair, looks more vividly out of the history
of his time than any other. For Castruccio had been in
prison, appointed to die, and when the rising of the Lucchese
delivered him, and made him Lord of Lucca, Uguccione's
fetters were still upon him. He was of the ancient Ghibelline
family of the Antelminelli, who had prospered to great
wealth in England, where they spent a long exile and where
Castruccio learned the art of war. After his death one of his
sons sold his dominion to another for twenty-two thousand

florins, from whom his German garrison took it and sold it for sixty thousand to Gherardo Spinola; he, in turn, disposed of it to the Rossi, at a clear loss of thirty-eight thousand florins. The Lucchese suffered six years under the Scaligeri, who sold them again – the market price this time is not quoted – to the Florentines, whom the Pisans drove out. These held her in a servitude so cruel that the Lucchese called it their Babylonian captivity, and when it was ended after twenty years, through the intervention of the Emperor Charles IV, in 1369, they were obliged to pay the German a hundred thousand florins for their liberty, which had been sold so many times for far less money.

An ancient Lucchese family, the Guanigi, whose Gothic palaces are still the most beautiful in the city, now rose to power, and held it till 1430; and then the city finally established the republican government, which in its democratic and oligarchic form continued till 1799.

The noblest event of this long period was the magnanimous attempt of the gonfaloniere, Francesco Burlamacchi, who in 1546 dreamed of driving the Medici from power and re-establishing the republic throughout Tuscany. Burlamacchi was of an old patrician family, but the love of freedom had been instilled in him by his uncle, Filippo Burlamacchi, that Fra Pacifico who wrote the first life of Savonarola and was one of his most fervent disciples. The gonfaloniere's plot was discovered; and he was arrested by the timid Lucchese Senate, which hastened to assure the ferocious Cosimo I. that they were guiltless of complicity. The imperial commissioner came from Milan to preside at his trial, and he was sentenced to suffer death for treason to the empire. He was taken to Milan and beheaded; but now he is the greatest name in Lucca, and his statue in the piazza, fronting her ancient communal palace, appeals to all who love freedom with the memory of his high intent. He died in the same cause which Savonarola laid down his life for, and not less generously.

Poor little Lucca had not even the courage to attempt to save him; but doubtless she would have tried if she had dared. She was under the special protection of the emperors, having paid Maximilian and then Charles V good round sums for the confirmation of her early liberties; and she was so anxious to be well with the latter, that when she was accused to him of favoring the new Lutheran heresy she hastened to persecute the Protestants with the same cowardice that she had shown in abandoning Burlamacchi.

It cost, indeed, no great effort to suppress the Protestant congregation at Lucca. Peter Martyr, its founder, had fled before, and was now a professor at Strasburg, whence he wrote a letter of severe upbraiding to the timorous flock who suffered themselves to be frightened back to Rome. Some of them would not renounce their faith, preferring exile, and of these, who emigrated by families, were the Burlamacchi, from whom the hero came. He had counted somewhat upon the spirit of the Reformation to help him in his design against the Medici, knowing it to be the spirit of freedom, but there is no one evidence that he was himself more a Protestant than Savonarola was.

Eight years after his death the constitution of Lucca was changed, and she fell under the rule of an aristocracy nicknamed the Lords of the Little Ring, from the narrow circle in which her senators succeeded one another. She had always been called Lucca the Industrious; in her safe subordination, she now worked and throve for two hundred and fifty years, till the French republicans came and toppled her oligarchy over at a touch. James Howell, writing one of his delightful letters from Florence in 1621, gives us some notion of Lucca as she appeared to the polite traveller of that day.

"There is a notable active little Republic towards the midst of Tuscany," he says, "called Lucca, which, in regard she is under the Emperour's protection, he dares not meddle with, though she lie as a Partridg under a Faulcon's wings, in relation to the grand Duke; besides there is another reason of the State why he meddles not with her, because she is more beneficial unto him now that she is free, and more industrious to support this freedom, than if she were become his vassal; for then it is probable she would grow more careless and idle, and so would not vent his comodities so soon, which she buys for ready mony, wherein most of her wealth consists. There is no State that winds the peny more nimbly and makes a quicker return."

Lasells, who visited Lucca a little earlier, tells us that it "hath thirty thousand Muskets or half Muskets in its Arsenal, eight thousand Pikes, two thousand Brest Pieces of Musket proof, and store of great Artillery. The whole State, for a need, can arm eighteen thousand men of service;" but Lucca appears to have become the joke and by-word of her neighbors more and more as time went on. At Florence they told of a prima-donna who, when she gesticulated in opera at Lucca, flung her arms beyond the borders of the republic. An ignominious peace, timid, selfish, prudent, was her condition from the time the aristocratic change took place. For two centuries she was preparing for that Bourbon despotism which characterized her even physically to my fancy. "An

absolute government," says my Lucchese guide-book, "but
of mild temper, which might have been more beneficent if it
had been inspired by views less narrow. Yet it was a notable
period of our history for municipal activity and for public
works, which in proportion to the smallness of the country
may also be called great; the city secured by vast and well-
planned defences against the inundations of the Serchio;
the country traversed in every direction by carriage-roads;
abundance of the best water for use and beauty brought to
the city by a monumental work of art; an ample highway
across the Apennines, to communicate with Modena and
Lombardy; bridges, ornamental and convenient, of stone
and iron."

### III.

Of mediæval Lucca I have kept freshest the sense of her
Gothic church architecture, with its delicate difference from
that of Pisa, which it resembles and excels. It is touched with
the Lombardic and Byzantine character, while keeping its
own; here are the pillars resting on the backs of lions and
leopards; here are the quaint mosaics in the façades. You see
the former in the cathedral, which is not signally remarkable, like that of Florence, or Siena, or Pisa, and the latter in
the beautiful old church of San Frediano, an Irish saint who
for some reason figured in Lucca; he was bishop there in the
fifth century, and the foundation of his church dates only a
century or two later. San Michele is an admirable example
of Lucchese gothic, and is more importantly placed than
any other church, in the very heart of the town opposite
the Palazzo Pretorio. This structure was dedicated to the

occupation of the Podestà of Lucca, in pursuance of the republic's high-languaged decree, recognizing the fact that "among the ornaments with which cities embellish themselves, the greatest expenditure should always be devoted to those where the deities are worshipped, the magistracy administers justice, and the people convenes." The Palazzo Pretorio is now the repository of a public archæological collection, and the memory of its original use has so utterly perished that the combined intellects of two policemen, whom we appealed to for information, could not assign to it any other function than that of lottery office, appointed by the late grand duke. The popular intellect at Lucca is not very vivid, so far as we tested it, and though willing, it is not quick. The *caffetiera* in whose restaurant we took breakfast, under the shadow of the Pretorian Palace walls, was as ignorant of its history as the policemen; but she was very amiable, and she had three pretty daughters in the bon-bon department, who looked the friendliest disposition to know about it if they could.

I speak of them at once, because I did not think the Lucchese generally such handsome people as the Pisans, and I wish to be generous before I am just. Why, indeed, should I be severe with the poor Lucchese in any way, even for their ignorance, when the infallible Baedeker himself speaks of the statue in the Piazza S. Michele as that of "S. Burlamacchi"? The hero thus canonized stood frowning down upon a grain and seed market when we went to offer him our homage, and the peasants thought we had come to buy, and could not understand why we should have only a minor curiosity about their wares. They took the wheat up in their brown hands to show us, and boasted of its superior quality. We said we were strangers, and explained that we. had no intention of putting in a crop of that sort; but they only laughed blankly. In spite of this prevailing ignorance, penetrating even to the Baedeker in our hands, Lucca was much tableted to the memory of her celebrities, especially her literary celebrities, who need tablets as greatly as any literary celebrities I know. There was one literary lady whose tablet I saw in a church, and whom the local Scientific and Literary Academy proclaimed "the marvel of her age" for her learning and her gifts in improvisation. The reader will readily identify her from this; or if he cannot, the greater shame to him; he might as well be a Lucchese.

> "All there are barrators, except Bontura;
> No into yes for money there is changed,"

says Dante of this Lucca in which I found an aspect of busy commonplace, an air of thrift and traffic, and in which I only feign to have discovered an indifference to finer things. I dare say Lucca is full of intelligence and polite learning; but she does not imbue her policemen and *caffetieras* with it, as Boston does. Yet I would willingly be at this moment in a town where I could step out and see an old Roman amphitheatre, built bodily up into the modern city, and showing its mighty ribs through the houses surrounding the market-place, – a market-place quaint beyond any other, with its tile-roofed stands and booths. There is much more silk in Lucca than in Boston, if we have the greater culture; and the oil of Lucca is sublime; and – yes, I will own it! – Lucca has the finer city wall. The town showed shabby and poor from the driveway along the top of this, for we saw the backyards and rears of the houses; but now and then we looked down into a stiff, formal, delicious palace garden, full of weather-beaten statues, old, bad, ridiculous, divinely dear and beautiful!

I cannot say that I have been hardly used, when I remember that I have seen such gardens as those; and I humbly confess it a privilege to have walked in the shadow of the Guanigi palaces at Lucca, in which the gothic seems to have done its best for a stately and lovely effect. I even climbed to the top of one of their towers, which I had wondered at ever since my first sight of Lucca because of the little grove it bore upon its crest. I asked the custodian of the palace what it was, and he said it was a little garden, which I suspected already. But I had a consuming desire to know what it looked like, and what Lucca looked like from it; and I asked him how high the tower was. He answered that it was four hundred feet high, which I doubted at first, but came to believe when I had made the ascent. I hated very much to go up that tower; but when the custodian said that an English lady eighty years old had gone up the week before, I said to myself that I would not be outdone by any old lady of eighty, and I went up. The trees were really rooted in little beds of earth up there, and had been growing for ten years; the people of the house sometimes took tea under them in the summer evenings.

This tower was one of three hundred and seventy in which Lucca abounded before the Guanigi levelled them. They were for the convenience of private warfare; the custodian showed me a little chamber near the top, where he pretended the garrison used to stay. I enjoyed his statement as much as if it were a fact, and I enjoyed still more the magnificent prospect of the city and country from the towers; the fertile plain with the hills all round, and distant mountains snow-cowned except to the south where the valley widened toward Florence; the multitudinous roofs and bell-towers of the city, which filled its walls full of human habitations, with no breadths of orchard and field as at Pisa and Siena.

The present Count Guanigi, so the custodian pretended, lives in another palace, and lets this in apartments; yon may have the finest for seventy-five dollars a year, with privilege of sky-garden. I did not think it dear, and I said so, though I did not visit any of the interiors and do not know what state the finest of them may be in.

We did, however, see one Lucchese palace throughout; the Palazzo Mansi, in which there is an admirable gallery of Dutch pictures inherited by the late marquis through a Dutch marriage made by one of his ancestors. The portrait of this lady, a gay, exuberant, eighteenth-century blonde, ornaments the wall of one of the gilded and tapestried rooms which form two sides of the palace court. From a third, standing in an arcaded passage, you look across this court, gray with the stone of which the edifice is built, to a rich brown mass of tiled roofs, and receive a perfect impression of the pride and state in which life was lived in the old days in Lucca. It is a palace in the classic taste; it is excellent in its way, and it expresses as no other sort of edifice can the splendors of an aristocracy, after it has ceased to be feudal and barbaric, and become elegant and municipal. What laced coats and bag-wigs, what hoops and feathers had not alighted from gilt coaches and sedan-chairs in that silent and empty court! I am glad to be plebeian and American, a citizen of this enormous democracy, but if I were strictly cross-examined, would I not like also to be a Lord of the Little Ring in Lucca, a marquis, and a Mansi?

# Pistoja, Prato and Fiesole

## I.

It was on the last day of March, after our return from Siena, that I ran out to Pistoja with my friend the artist. There were now many signs of spring in the landscape, and the gray olives were a less prevalent tone, amid the tints of the peach and pear blossoms. Dandelions thickly strewed the railroad-sides; the grass was powdered with the little daisies, white with crimson-tipped petals; the garden-borders were full of yellow flowering seed-turnips. The peasants were spading their fields; as we ran along, it came noon, and they began to troop over the white roads to dinner, past villas frescoed with false balconies and casements, and comfortable brownish-gray farmsteads. On our right the waves of distant purple hills swept all the way to Pistoja.

I made it part of my business there to look up a young married couple, Americans, journeying from Venice to Florence, who stopped at Pistoja twenty years before, and saw the gray town in the gray light of a spring morning between four and six o'clock. I remembered how strange and beautiful they thought it, and from time to time I started with recognition of different objects — as if I had been one of that pair; so young, so simple-heartedly, greedily glad of all that eld and story which Italy constantly lavished upon them. I could not find them, but I found phantom traces of their youth in the ancient town, and that endeared it to me, and made it lovely through every hour of the long rainy day I spent there. To other eyes it might have seemed merely a stony old town, dull and cold under the lowering sky, with a locked-up cathedral, a bare baptistery, and a mediæval public palace, and a history early merged in that of Florence; but to me it must always have the tender interest of the pleasure, pathetically intense, which that young couple took in it. They were very hungry, and they could get no breakfast in the drowsy town, not even a cup of coffee, but they did not mind that; they wandered about, famished but blest, and by one of the happy accidents that usually befriended them, they found their way up to the Piazza del Duomo and saw the Communal Palace so thoroughly, in all its gothic fulness and mediæval richness of detail, that I seemed never to have risen from the stone benching around the interior of the court on which they sat to study the escutcheons carven and painted on the walls. I could swear that the bear on the arms of Pistoja was the same that they saw and noted with the amusement which a bear in a checkered tabard must inspire in ignorant minds; though I am now able to inform the reader that it was put there because Pistoja was anciently infested with bears, and this was the last bear left when they were exterminated.

We need not otherwise go deeply into the history of Pistoja. We know already how one of her family feuds introduced the factions of the Bianchi and Neri in Florence, and finally caused the exile of Dante; and we may inoffensively remember that Cataline met his defeat and death on her hills A. U. 691. She was ruled more or less tumultuously by princes, popes, and people till the time of her great siege by the Lucchese and Florentines and her own Guelph exiles in 1305. Famine began to madden the besieged, and men and women stole out of the city through the enemy's camp and scoured the country for food. When the Florentines found this out they lay in wait for them, and such as they caught they mutilated, cutting off their noses, or arms, or legs, and then exposing them to the sight of those they had gone out to save from starvation. After the city fell the Florentine and Lucchese leaders commanded such of the wounded Pistojese as they found on the field to be gathered in heaps upon the demolished walls, that their fathers, brothers, and children might see them slowly die, and forbade any one, under pain of a like fate, to succor one of these miserable creatures.

Pistoja could not endure the yoke fastened upon her. A few years later her whole people rose literally in a frenzy of rebellion against the Lucchese governor, and men, women, children, priests, and monks joined in driving him out. After the heroic struggle they re-established their own republic, which presently fell a prey to the feud of two of her families, in whose private warfare she suffered almost as much as from her foreign enemies. Between them the Cancellieri and the Panciatichi burned a thousand houses within her walls, not counting those without, and the latter had plotted to deliver over their country to the Visconti of Milan, when the Florentines intervened and took final possession of Pistoja.

We had, therefore, not even to say that we were of the Cancellieri party in order to enter Pistoja, but drove up to the Hotel di Londra without challenge, and had dinner there, after which we repaired to the Piazza del Duomo; and while the artist got out a plate and began to etch in the rain, the author bestirred himself to find the sacristan and get into the cathedral. It was easy enough to find the sacristan, but when he had been made to put his head out of the fifth-story window he answered, with a want of enterprise and hospitality which I had never before met in Italy, that the cathedral was always open at three o'clock, and he would not come down to open it sooner. At that hour I revenged myself upon him by not finding it very interesting, though I think now the fault must have been in me. There is enough estimable detail of art, especially the fourteenth-century monument to the great lawyer and lover, Cino da Pistoja, who is represented lecturing to Petrarch among eight other of his pupils. The lady in the group is the Selvaggia whom he immortalized in his subtle and metaphysical verses; she was the daughter of Filippo Vergiolesi, the leader of the Ghibellines in Pistoja, and she died of hopeless love for Cino, when the calamities of their country drove him into exile at the time of the siege. He remains the most tangible if not the greatest name of Pistoja; he was the first of those who polished the Tuscan speech; he was a wonder of jurisprudence in his time, restoring the Roman law and commenting nine books of the Code; and the wayfarer, whether grammarian, attorney, litterateur, or young lady may well look on his monument with sympathy.

But I brought away no impression of pleasure or surprise from the cathedral generally, and in fact the works of art for which one may chiefly, if not solely, desire to see Pistoja again, are the Della Robbias, which immortally beautify the Ospedale del Ceppo. They represent with the simplest reality, and in the proportions of life, the seven works of mercy of St. Andrea Franchi, bishop of Pistoja, in 1399. They form a frieze or band round the edifice, and are of the glazed terra cotta in which the Della Robbias commonly wrought. The saint is seen visiting "The Naked," "The Pilgrims," "The Sick," "The Imprisoned," "The Dead," "The An Hungered," "The Athirst;" and between the tableaux are the figures of "Faith," "Charity," "Hope," "Prudence," and "Justica." There is also "An Annunciation," "A Visitation," "An Assumption;" and in three circular reliefs, adorned with fruits and flowers after the Della Robbia manner, the arms of the hospital, the city, and the Medici; but what takes the eye and the heart are the good bishop's works of mercy. In these color is used as it must be in that material, and in the broad, unmingled blues, reds, yellows, and greens, primary, sincere, you have satisfying actuality of effect. I believe the critics are not decided that these are the best works of the masters, but they gave me more pleasure than any others, and I remember them with a vivid joy still. It is hardly less than startling to see them first, and then for every succeeding moment it is delightful. Giovanni della Robbia and his brother, the monk Frate Ambrogio, and Andrea and his two sons, Luca and Girolomo, are all supposed to have shared in this work, which has, therefore, a peculiar interest, though it is not even mentioned by Vasari, and seems to have suffered neglect by all the earlier connoisseurs. It was skilfully restored in 1826 by a Pistojese architect, who removed the layer of dust that had hardened upon the glaze and hid the colors; and in 1839 the French Government asked leave to reproduce it in plaster for the Beaux Arts; from which copy another was made for the Crystal Palace at Sydenham. It is, by all odds, the chiefest thing in Pistoja, where the reader, when he goes to look at it, may like to recall the pretty legend of the dry treestump (*ceppo*) breaking into bud and leaf, to indicate to the two good Pistojese of six hundred years ago where to found the hospital which this lovely frieze adorns.

Apparently, however, Pistoja does not expect to be visited for this or any other reason. I have already held up to obloquy the want of public spirit in the sacristan of the cathedral, and I have now to report an equal indifference on the part of the owner of a beautiful show-villa which a cabman persuaded me drive some miles out of the town through the rain to see. When we reached its gate, we were told that the villa was closed; simply that — closed. But I was not wholly a loser, for in celebration of my supposed disappointment my driver dramatized a grief which was as fine a theatrical spectacle as I have seen.

Besides, I was able to stop on the way back at the ancient church of Sant' Andrea, where I found myself as little expected, indeed, as elsewhere, but very prettily welcomed by the daughter of the sacristan, whose father was absent, and who made me free of the church. I thought that I wished to see the famous pulpit of Giovanna da Pisa, son of Niccolò, and the little maid had to light me a candle to look at it with. She was not of much help otherwise; she did not at all understand the subjects, neither the Nativity, nor the Adoration of the Magi ("Who were the three Magi Kings?" she asked, and was so glad when I explained), nor the Slaughter of the Innocents, nor the Crucifixion, nor the Judgment. These facts were as strange to her as the marvellous richness and delicacy of the whole work, which, for opulence of invention and perfect expression of intention, is surely one of the most wonderful things in all that wonderland of Italy. She stood by and freshly admired, while I lectured her upon it as if I had been the sacristan and she a simple maid from America, and got the hot wax of the candle all over my fingers.

She affected to refuse my fee. "*Le pare!*" she said, with the sweetest pretence of astonishment (which, being interpreted, is something like "The idea!"); and when I forced the coin into her unwilling hand, she asked me to come again, when her father was at home.

Would I could! There is no such pulpit in America, that I know of; and even Pistoja, in the rain and mud, nonchalant, unenterprising, is no bad placa.

I had actually business there besides that of a scribbling dilletante, and it took me, on behalf of a sculptor who had some medallions casting, to the most ancient of the several bronze foundries in Pistoja. This foundry, an irregular group of low roofs, was enclosed in a hedge of myrtle, and I descended through flowery garden-paths to the office, where the master met me with the air of a host, instead of that terrifying no-admittance-except-on-business address, which I have encountered in my rare visits to foundries in my own country. Nothing could have been more fascinating than the interior of the workshop, in which the bronze figures, groups, reliefs, stood about in every variety of dimension and all stages of finish. When I confessed my ignorance, with a candor which I shall not expect from the reader, of how the sculpturesque forms to their last fragile and delicate detail were reproduced in metal, he explained that an exact copy was first made in wax, which was painted with successive coats of liquid mud, one dried upon another, till a sufficient thickness was secured, and then the wax was melted out, and the bronze was poured in.

I said how very simple it was when one knew, and he said, yes, very simple; and I came away sighing for the day when our foundries shall be enclosed in myrtle hedges, and reached through gardenpaths. I suppose I shall hardly see it, however, for it had taken almost a thousand years for that foundry in Pisa to attain its idyllic setting. Patience!

## II.

On my way home from Lucca, I stopped at Prato, whither I had been tempted to go all winter by the steam-tramway trains snuffling in and out of our Piazza Santa Maria Novella at Florence. I found it a flat, dull, commonplace-looking town at first blush, with one wild, huge, gaunt piazza, planted with straggling sycamores, and banged all round by copper-smiths, whose shops seemed to alternate with the stables occupying its arcades. Multitudinous hanks of new-dyed yarn blew in the wind under the trees, and through all the windows and open doors I saw girls and women plaiting straw. This forms the chief industry of Prato, where, as a kind little priest with a fine Roman profile, in the railway carriage, assured me between the prayers he kept saying to himself, there was work for all and all were at work.

Secular report was not so flattering to Prato. I was told that business was but dull there since the death of the English gentleman, one Mr. Askew, who has done so much for it, and who lies buried in the odor of sanctity in the old Carmelite convent. I saw his grave there when I went to look at the frescos, under the tutelage of an old, sleek, fat monk, roundest of the round dozen of brothers remaining since the suppression. I cannot say now why I went to see these frescos, but I must have been told by some local guide they were worthy to be seen, for I find no mention of them in the books. My old monk admired them without stint, and had a particular delight in the murder of St. Martin, who was stabbed in the back at the altar.

He rubbed his hands gleefully and pointed out the flying acolyte: *"Sempre scappa, ma è sempre là!"* (Always running, but always there!) And then he burst into a childish, simple laugh that was rather grewsome, considering its inspiration and the place.

Upon the whole, it might have been as well to suppress that brother along with the convent; though I was glad to hear his praises of the Englishman who had befriended the little town so wisely; and I was not troubled to learn that this good man was a convert to the religion of his beneficiaries.

All that I ever knew of him I heard from the monk and read from his gravestone; but until he came nothing so definite had been done, probably, to mend the prosperity of Prato, broken by the sack in 1512, when the Spaniards, retiring from their defeat at Ravenna by Gaston de Foix, sat down before the town and pounded a hole in its undefended wall with their cannon. They were the soldiers of that Holy League which Pope Julius II. invented, and they were marching upon Florence to restore the Medici. They were very hungry, and as fearless as they were pitiless; and when they had made a breach in the wall, they poured into the town and began to burn and to kill, to rob and to ravish.

"Five thousand persons," says a careful and temperate history, "without resisting, without defending themselves, without provocation, were inhumanly slaughtered in cold

blood; neither age nor sex was spared, nor sanctity re-
spected; every house, every church, every convent was
pillaged, devastated, and brutally defiled. Only the cathedral, thanks to the safeguard posted there by the Cardinal
Legate Giovanni de Medici, was spared, and this was filled
with women, gathered there to weep, to pray, to prepare
for death. For days the barbarous soldiery rioted in the
sack of the hapless city, which, with its people decimated
and its territory ravaged, never fully rose again from its
calamity; more than three centuries passed before its population reached the number it had attained before the siege."

At that time Prato had long been subject to Florence,
but in its day Prato had also been a free and independent
republic, with its factions and its family feuds, like another.
The greatest of its families were the Guazziolitri, of Guelph
politics, who aspired to its sovereignty, but were driven
out and all their property confiscated. They had built for
their palace and fortress the beautiful old pile which now
serves the town for municipal uses, and where there is an
interesting little gallery, though one ought rather to visit it
for its own sake, and the stately image it keeps in singular
perfection of a grandeur of which we can now but dimly
conceive.

I said that Prato was dull and commonplace, but that
only shows how pampered and spoiled one becomes by
sojourn in Italy. Let me explain now that it was only dull
and commonplace in comparison with other towns I had
been seeing. If we had Prato in America we might well visit
it for inspiration from its wealth of picturesqueness, and
history, and of art. We have, of course, nothing to compare
with it; and one ought always to remember, in reading the

notes of the supercilious American tourist in Italy, that he is sneering with a mental reservation to this effect. More memory, more art, more beauty clusters about the Duomo at Prato than about – I do not wish to be extravagant – the New Old South in Boston or Grace Church in New York.

I am afraid, indeed, we should not find in the interior even of these edifices such frescos as those of Lippo Lippi and Ghirlandajo in the cathedral at Prato; and as for the Della Robbia over the door and the pulpit of Donatello on the corner without, where they show the Virgin's girdle on her holiday, what shall one say? We have not even a girdle of the Virgin! These are the facts that must still keep us modest and make us beg not to be taken too positively, when we say Prato is not interesting. In that pulpit, with its "marble brede" of dancing children, one sees almost at his best a sculptor whose work, after that of Mino da Fiesole, goes most to the heart of the beholder.

I hung about the piazza, delighting in it, till it was time to take the steam-tramway to Florence, and then I got the local postman to carry my bag to the cars for me. He was the gentlest of postmen, and the most grateful for my franc, and he explained as we walked how he was allowed by the Government to make what sums he could in this way between his distributions of the mail. His salary was fifty francs a month, and he had a family.

I dare say he is removed by this time, for a man with an income like that must seem an Offensive Partisan to many people of opposite politics in Prato.

The steam-tramway train consisted of two or three horse-cars coupled together, and drawn by the pony-engine I was familiar with in our Piazza. This is a common means of travel between all large Italian cities and outlying small towns, and I wonder why we have not adopted it in America. We rattled pleasantly along the level of the highway at the rate of ten or twelve miles an hour, and none of the horses seemed to be troubled by us. They had probably been educated up to the steam-tram, and I will never believe that American horses are less capable of intellectual development than the Italian.

### III.

We postponed our visit to Fiesole, which we had been meaning to make all winter, until the last days of our Florentine sojourn, and it was quite the middle of April when we drove up to the Etruscan city.

"Go by the new road and come back by the old," said a friend who heard we were really going at last. "Then you will get the whole thing."

We did so; but I am not going to make the reader a partner of all of our advantages; I am not sure that he would be grateful for them; and to tell the truth, I have forgotten which road Boccaccio's villa was on and which the villa of the Medici. Wherever they are they are charming. The villa of Boccaccio is now the Villa Palmieri; I still see it fenced with cypresses, and its broad terrace peopled with weather-beaten statues, which at a distance I could not have sworn were not the gay ladies and gentlemen who met there and told their merry tales while the plague raged in Florence. It is not only famous as the supposed scene of the Decamerone; but it takes its name from a learned gentleman who wrote a poem there, in which he maintained that at the time of Satan's rebellion the angels who remained neutral became the souls now inhabiting our bodies. For this uncomfortable doctrine his poem, though never printed, was condemned by the Inquisition – and justly. The Villa Medici, once Villa Mozzi, and now called Villa Spence, after the English gentleman who inhabits it, was the favorite seat of Lorenzo before he placed himself at Villa Carreggi; hither he resorted with his wits, his philosophers, his concubines, buffoons, and scholars; and here it was that the Pazzi hoped to have killed him and Giuliano at the time of their ill-starred conspiracy. You come suddenly upon it, deeply dropped amidst its gardens, at a turn of the winding slopes which make the ascent to Fiesole a constantly changing delight and wonder.

Fiesole was farther than she seemed in the fine, high air she breathes, and we had some long hours of sun and breeze in the exquisite spring morning before the first Etruscan emissaries met us with the straw fans and parasols whose fabrication still employs their remote antiquity. They were pretty children and young girls, and they were preferable to the mediæval beggars who had swarmed upon us at the first town outside the Florentine limits, whither the Pia Casa di Recovero could not reach them. From every point the world-old town, fast seated on its rock, looked like a fortress, inexpugnable and picturesque; but it kept neither promise, for it yielded to us without a struggle, and then was rather tame and commonplace, – commonplace and tame, of course, comparatively. It is not everywhere that you have an impressive Etruscan wall; a grassgrown Roman amphitheatre, lovely, silent; a museum stocked with classic relics and a custodian with a private store of them for sale, not to speak of a cathedral begun by the Florentines just after they destroyed Fiesole in 1000. Fiesole certainly does not, however, invite one by its modern aspect to think of the Etruscan capital which Cicero attacked in the Roman Senate for the luxury of its banquets and the lavish display of its inhabitants. It was but a plain and simple repast that the Caffè Aurora afforded us, and the Fiesolans seemed a plain and simple folk; perhaps in one of them who was tipsy an image of their classic corruptions survived.

The only excitement of the place we seemed to have brought with us; there had, indeed, been an election some time before, and the dead walls — it seems odd that all the walls in Fiesole should not be dead by this time — were still placarded with appeals to the enlightened voters to cast their ballots for Peruzzi, candidate for the House of Deputies and a name almost as immemorial as their town's.

However luxurious, the Fiesolans were not proud; a throng of them followed us into the cathedral, where we went to see the beautiful monument of Bishop Salutali by Mino da Fiesole, and allowed me to pay the sacristan for them all. There may have been a sort of justice in this; they must have seen the monument so very often before!

They were sociable, but not obtrusive, not even at the point called the Belvedere, where, having seen that we were already superabundantly supplied with straw fans and parasols, they stood sweetly aside and enjoyed our pleasure in the views of Florence. This ineffable prospect —

But let me rather stand aside with the Fiesolans, and leave it to the reader!